For
George
in friendship

Stuart Brent

"Stuart Brent is the Orpheus of Chicago booksellers, ready to challenge hell itself to bring a beautiful book back to Chicago and the light of its reading lamps."

—Saul Bellow

"Stuart Brent is more than Chicago's premier bookseller. For more than 40 years he has been cheerleader and nurse of Chicago's writers. In 1947 I first went to The Seven Stairs and found what was for me a dream of bohemian intellectual life, and going into his store still brings out the wide-eyed boy in me."

—Allan Bloom

•

THE SEVEN STAIRS

by Stuart Brent

A TOUCHSTONE BOOK
Published by Simon & Schuster Inc.
NEW YORK · LONDON · TORONTO · SYDNEY · TOKYO

Touchstone
Simon & Schuster Building
Rockefeller Center
1230 Avenue of the Americas
New York, New York 10020

10 9 8 7 6 5 4 3 2 1 Pbk.

Library of Congress Cataloging in Publication data
Brent, Stuart.
    The Seven Stairs / by Stuart Brent.—1st Touchstone ed.

        p.   cm.—(A Touchstone book)
    Reprint. Originally published: Boston : Houghton Mifflin, 1962.
    1. Brent, Stuart.   2. Booksellers and bookselling—Illinois—
Chicago—History—20th century.   3. Booksellers and bookselling—
United States—Biography.   4. Chicago (Ill.)—Intellectual
life—20th century.   I. Title.
Z473.B795A3   1989
070.5′092′4—dc 19   89-30410
[B]   CIP
ISBN 0-671-67394-7 Pbk.

To
my
mother
and
father

Contents

Preface

The Seven Stairs, a memoir first published in 1962 by Houghton Mifflin Company, Boston, was reprinted in a paperback edition in 1973. Both editions have long been out of print. Modern books, of course, disappear from the scene rather quickly, even those with qualities that could bring joy and satisfaction to succeeding generations of readers. Being published today is a poor means for gaining immortality. Even the paper won't last very long.

For a book to come into being and reach its potential audience, a collaboration must take place among a number of individuals, all of whom may be regarded as endangered species: a perceptive editor, a responsible publisher, and finally, a bookseller who communicates personally with book buyers. Without this chain of sponsorship, it will be difficult, if not impossible, to sustain a literature of enduring value.

The Seven Stairs was the name of the bookshop on Rush Street in Chicago which I opened in 1946 on a G.I. loan for three hundred dollars and a pocketful of dreams.

Actually, the Seven Stairs didn't last long. I had to move to Michigan Avenue where there were enough shoppers to sustain a business. But everything that was important about the propagation of the printed word as a vital force came into focus for me at that time.

Most of the things that I learned to value are being systematically undermined in an economy based on the "bottom line" and a culture devoted to the coarsening of taste. But I have never lost faith in bookselling as my calling. Quite often I feel as though I am crying in the wilderness. Then I remember the words that long ago inspired the defenders of Masada: "Know before whom ye stand." When I look at the faces of young people who come into the store, I ask myself, "Why are they so sad?" It then seems to me that it is worth being a defender of the faith. A new printing of *The Seven Stairs* is primarily for them.

Kafka was right. "A book should be the ax for the frozen sea within us." We cannot let good books die out or willingly leave behind us a legacy of meaningless despair. Whatever we can do to rekindle the passion for literature is worth everything.

As recounted in these pages, the late Ben Hecht used to thrill me with his tales of a Chicago literary scene that no longer existed, yet colored and excited my perception of my own days and ways and of the trials of my contemporaries in consorting with the Muse.

Dr. Daniel L. Boorstin, Jr. has attributed the national malaise to "our imprisonment in the present." The young writer today needs the comfort of F. Scott Fitzgerald's words of introduction to his masterpiece, *The Great Gatsby:* "But remember, also young man, you are not the first person who has been alone and alone." He needs to be stirred by the continuing possibilities of human achievement. There is such a sad gulf between Stephen Spender's poem beginning "I think continually of those who were truly great" and Allen Ginsberg's "I have seen the best minds of my generation destroyed by madness, starving hysterical naked, dragging themselves through the negro streets at dawn looking for an angry fix . . ."

Spender was writing in the 1930's when the world was falling apart. Ginsberg's "Howl" was the manifesto of alienated youth in an age of affluence.

Each generation requires not only the sense of its own newness, but also strength derived from fellowship with those who came before. Libraries, bookstores, even the memoirs of bookmen, may be justified to the degree that they administer to this sense of continuity.

I have never lost my naïve faith in the necessity for selling good books. Time and again, only innocence and ignorance have saved me. Had I ever given in to external reality, my world would surely have collapsed.

So here it is, the world that was, of the Seven Stairs, reprinted without alteration, except for a few egregious errors and lapses into my propensity for automatic writing.

STUART BRENT

Acknowledgments

I<small>N A</small> real sense, this book is an acknowledgment to all who have had a part in shaping my life and being. Since their names appear only incidentally and accidentally—if at all—in the course of the text, I hope with all my heart that they will accept this collective note of gratitude for all their help.

In particular, however, I wish to mention Hardwick Moseley for his encouragement when the going was rough; Milton Gilbert who made the Seven Stairs possible in the first place; Henry Dry, one of the few men I know who understand the meaning of forbearance; Goldie and Kalmin Levin (Jennie's mother and father) for their devotion and unfailing help; Robert Parrish for his blue penciling; and Hope, who after giving birth to our son, Joseph, tenderly cared for the unstrung father through the pangs of giving birth to *The Seven Stairs*.

S. B.

THE

SEVEN

STAIRS

1

And Nobody Came

I MIGHT as well tell you what this book is about.

Years ago I started to write a memoir about a young fellow who wanted to be a book dealer and how he made out. I tore it up when I discovered the subject had already been covered by a humorist named Will Cuppy in a book called, *How to Become Extinct*.

Now I'm. not so sure. I'm still around in my middle-aged obsolescence and all about us the young are withering on the vine. Civilization may beat me yet in achieving the state of the dodo. The tragedy is that so few seem to know or really believe it. Maybe there just isn't enough innocence left to join with the howl of the stricken book dealer upon barging into the trap. Not just a howl of self-pity, but the yap of the human spirit determined to assert itself no matter what. There's some juice in that spirit yet, or there would be no point in submitting the following pages as supporting evidence — hopefully, or bitterly, or both.

Let there be no doubt about my original qualifications for the role of Candide. With three hundred dollars worth of books (barely enough to fill five shelves), a used record player, and some old recordings (left in my apartment when I went into the army and still there upon my return), I opened the Seven Stairs Book and Record Shop on the Near North Side of Chicago.

The shop was located in one of the old brownstone, converted residences still remaining on Rush Street — a fashionable townhouse district in the era after the Great Chicago Fire, now the kind of a district into which fashionable townhouses inevitably decline. One had to climb a short flight of stairs above an English basement (I thought there were seven steps — in reality there were eight), pass through a short, dark hall, and unlock a door with a dime store skeleton key before entering finally into the prospective shop. It was mid-August of 1946 when I first stood there in the barren room. The sun had beaten in all day and I gasped for air; and gasping, I stood wondering if this was to be the beginning of a new life and an end to the hit-or-miss of neither success nor failure that summed up my career to the moment.

It all fitted my mood perfectly: the holes in the plaster, the ripped molding, the 1890 light fixture that hung by blackened chains from the ceiling, the wood-burning fireplace, the worn floor, the general air of decay lurking in every corner. Long before the scene registered fully upon my mind, it had entered into my emotions. I saw everything and forgave everything. It could all be repaired, painted, cleaned — set right with a little work. I saw the little room filled with books and records, a fire going, and myself in a velvet jacket, seated behind a desk, being charming and gracious to everyone who came in.

I saw success, excitement, adventure, in the world I loved — the world of books and music. I saw fine people coming and going — beautiful women and handsome men. I saw myself surrounded by warmth, friendship and good feeling, playing my favorite recordings all day, telling my favorite stories, finding myself.

I ran my fingers over the mantelpiece. "I want this room," I said to myself. "I want it."

I built shelves to the ceiling and bought all the books I could buy. There was no money left to buy the velvet jacket. Every morning I opened the store bright and early. Every night I closed very late. And no one came to visit me. Morning, noon, and night it was the same. I was alone with my books and my music. Everything was so bright, so shiny, so clean. And the books! There were not very many, but they were all so good! Still nobody came.

How do you go about getting people to buy books? I didn't know. I had been a teacher before the war. My father was not a businessman either, nor his father. No one in my family knew anything about business. I knew the very least.

Every morning I walked into the shop freshly determined: today I will sell a book! I hurried with my housekeeping. And then, what to do? Phone a friend or a relative. I couldn't think of a relative who read or a friend who wouldn't see through the thin disguise of my casual greeting and understand the ulterior purpose of my call.

One late afternoon it happened. One of the beautiful people I had dreamed about *came in.*

She stood on the threshold, apparently debating whether it was safe to venture further. "Is this a bookstore?" she said.

"Please come in," I said. "It's a bookshop."

She was solidly built and had a round face above a heavy neck with the fat comfortably overlapping the collar of her white dress. Her legs were sturdy, her feet were spread in a firm stance, she was fat and strong and daring.

"Do you have a copy of *Peace of Mind?*" said my daring first customer.

Everyone was reading the rabbi's book that summer — except me. It was a bestseller; naturally I wouldn't touch it. But here was a customer!

"Lady," I said, opening my business career on a note of total capitulation, "if you'll wait here a moment, I'll get the book for you." She nodded.

"Please," I added, running out the door.

I sprinted four blocks to A. C. McClurg's, the wholesaler from whom I bought my original three hundred dollars' worth of books, and bought a single copy of *Peace of Mind* for $1.62. Then I ran back to complete my first sale for $2.50.

The realization overwhelmed me that I was totally unprepared to sell a book. I had no bags or wrapping paper. I had no cash register or even a cigar box. It seemed highly improper to accept money and then reach into my pocket for change. It was a long time, in fact, before I could get over the embarrassment of taking anyone's money at all. I found it very upsetting.

2

"Read Your Lease. Goodbye."

THE NEAR North Side of Chicago is a Greenwich Village, a slum, and a night life strip bordered by the commerce of Michigan Avenue and the Gold Coast homes and apartments of the wealthy.

Into a narrow trough between the down-and-out losers of Clark Street and the luxurious livers of Lake Shore Drive flows a stream of life that has no direction, organization, or established pattern. Here are attracted the inner-directed ones struggling with their own visions, along with the hangers-on, the disenchanted and emotionally bankrupt. It is a haven for the broken soul as well as the earnest and rebellious. The drug addict, the petty thief, the sex deviant and the alcoholic are generously mixed in among the sincere and aspiring. There are the dislocated wealthy, the connivers and parasites, abortionists and pimps. There are call girls and crowds of visiting firemen, second hand clothing stores and smart shops, pawn brokers and art supply stores.

Gertrude Stein once wrote abou. Picasso's reply to a young man who was seeking advice on the best location for opening a Parisian bookstore: "I would just find a place and start selling books." Well, I found a place, uniquely unfavored as a crossroads of commerce (during the day, virtually no one was on the street), but teeming with the malcontents, the broken, the battered — the flotsam and jetsam of urban life, along with inspired or aspiring prophets, musicians, artists, and writers. What more could one ask?

The original dimensions of the Seven Stairs were fifteen feet by nine feet. A single bay window looked onto Rush Street. At the other end of the room stood a small sink. The bathroom was on the second floor and seldom worked. Three ashcans on the sidewalk by my window served the building for garbage disposal. Occasionally the city emptied them.

Across the hall was a hat shop — a blind for a call girl establishment. The woman who ran it was actually a hat maker and made hats for her girls. She was a heavy woman with enormous breasts, who wore immense earrings, always dressed in black silk, and changed her hair dye regularly: red, jet black, once silver-grey. She had a small, bow-shaped mouth, garishly painted, and in the four years I knew her an improper word never passed her lips. She was filled with commiseration for cats, at least a dozen of which wandered in and out of the hall daily. Once in a while, she would buy a book, always with a fifty dollar bill, and then was very apologetic for the inconvenience when I had to run to the drug store for change.

Behind my shop was another studio occupied by a charming hypochondriacal ballet dancer and a boy-friend who was the tallest, ugliest man I had ever encountered. Above were two more studios, occupied by a painter and a girl who wrote poetry. There were also two studios on the third floor, but to this day I have no idea who was there. A bricklayer lived in the basement with his odd and rather pretty daughter, who had bad teeth, a nervous tic, and huge, burning black eyes.

Over this assortment of humanity ruled an evil king who in my reasoned opinion was in fact Mephistopheles in the guise of a landlord. His life had its meaning in seeing that the innocent were punished, that neighbors were aroused to hate and distrust one another, and that needless disaster always threatened his subjects and often befell them.

It was amazing how he could achieve his devilish ends by the simple incantation, "Read your lease. Goodbye." This was his message, whether in the inevitable phone call when you were a day late with the rent, or in answer to your call for help when the fuses in the basement blew or when on a bitter February night the sink broke and the shop began floating away.

The sink affair occurred at a point when my business had developed to the extent of a few regular accounts and come to a quiet stalemate. Once these faithful customers had come in, I was through for the month. I could scarcely stand the empty hours waiting for someone to talk with. It was bitter February, cold enough to keep any sensible soul off the streets. I sat before the fire, filled with self-pity, my doomed life stretching hopelessly before me.

Finally I bestirred myself — and this was my undoing.

All I did was throw a carton up to a shelf — a sort of basketball toss that missed. The box hit the sink, tipped off, and, incredibly, broke an aged lead water pipe. To my horror, water began gushing over the floor. I tried to stuff a towel into the pipe. No good. My beautiful shop! All the beautiful books! Ruin!

Still holding the towel to the pipe with one hand, I dialed my father's telephone number. He was a sound man concerning the mechanical world.

"Do you have a broom?" he said. "All right, cut it in two and make a plug for the pipe. Then call your landlord."

I went to work frantically. All the time water was pouring across the floor. Finally I managed to whittle a temporary plug. Then I phoned the landlord.

He inquired of my business success.

"Please," I said. "The pipe to the sink has broken. My store will be ruined. Where is the shut-off?"

"I don't know where the shut-off is," he said. "You are responsible. Read your lease. Goodbye."

I turned to the City Water Department next. By the time I explained to them what had happened and they examined their charts and discovered where the cut-offs might be located, I was standing in an inch of water.

Someone would be over, I was assured. But not right away. In a few hours perhaps. All the men were out on emergencies. However, I could try to find the cut-offs myself. They were outside near the street lamp about a foot from the curb.

I stuck my head out the door. It was about ten degrees above zero, and the ground along the curbing was covered with at least five inches of ice and snow. What to do? And all the time, more water was bubbling over the broom handle and splashing onto the floor.

Down at the corner there was a drug store owned by a man of infinite patience and understanding. No human act was beyond his comprehension or forgiveness, and he was always ready to help in moments of crisis. If a girl needed help, our man at the drug store was there. If she needed work, legitimate or otherwise, he could find the spot for her. If a man needed to make a touch, he could get it without interest. Our druggist was no fence or law breaker — but he was an answering service, a father confessor, and an unlikely guardian angel. I ran to him with my trouble.

He looked at me with his sleepy eyes, and, his soft lips forming quiet assurances, came up with a shovel, an ax, and a pail of hot water.

The problem was where to dig. I went at it blindly, saying to myself: "Shovel. Shovel. Die if you must. But shovel."

When I had gotten an area of snow removed, I poured water over the ice and went at it with the ax. Finally I struck the top of the box containing the cut-offs and managed to pry open the lid. There were two knobs in the box, and having no idea which one related to my store, I turned them both shut.

After returning the hardware to the drug store, I sloshed back into my inundated establishment and began sweeping the water out with what was left of the broom. Working like a madman, I got most of the water out into the hall, out the door, and over the stairs, where it froze instantaneously. Never mind — tomorrow I will chop the ice away and all will be well.

By this time, my strength was exhausted and the shop was nearly as cold as the outdoors. I felt as though I had survived some kind of monstrous test. I dumped logs on the fire, waited until they were ablaze, then stripped off my wet shoes and socks and wrapped my frozen feet in my coat.

I was sure I had caught pneumonia. I wouldn't be able to open the store for weeks. The few accounts I had would surely be lost. It was the end of everything. How good it would be if only death would come now, while there was yet a little warmth to taste in a world which certainly wanted nothing of my kind.

Out of my reverie, I heard a bitter cry. It came from outside near my door. I jumped up and looked down the hall. Two men in evening dress were wrestling on the stairs. The screaming and cursing were awful. At last they scrambled up and started toward me.

"You son of a bitch," one of them cried. "I'll kill you!" His fall on the stairs had damaged his suit. Bits of ice had collected about his long nose, a few even glistened in his moustache. His hair practically stood on end. Snow and ice covered his jacket and patched his trousers. His black tie was crooked and his dress shirt sodden. The other fellow stared fiercely at me, restraining his partner with one hand, the other balled into a fist, threatening me. "Who put you up to this? Why do you want to ruin our

business? You mother-raping bastard, I'll cut your
throat!" He took a step forward. I stepped back.

"Tell us or we'll kill you here and now."

I had never seen these men before in my life. As I retreated toward my desk, they swept the books off it onto
the wet floor. They sat on the desk and stared at me, and
everything became very quiet.

They were proprietors of the restaurant in the corner
building, also owned by my landlord. In shutting off the
water, I had turned off theirs, too. They also had called
the landlord, and he told them that I was undoubtedly responsible. But he failed to tell them what had been happening to me.

Now I showed them the broken pipe, the floor still wet
in spots, my hands which were raw and bruised. I picked
up the books from the floor and took off the wet dust jackets. Here goes my profit for a week, I thought. I could tell
their anger had cooled. Instead of being cruel, they
looked almost contrite. I went outside again in my wet
shoes and socks and coat and turned one of the shut-off
keys. Naturally it was the wrong one. The restaurant
man pounded at the window to attract my attention. I
reversed my switches and restored their precious water.

I remained in the shop a while, too exhausted and
heartbroken to leave. Where now, little man? I didn't
know. But I resolved never to call my landlord again — no
matter what.

It was a fruitless resolve. One morning two inspectors
from the Fire Department paid me a visit.

"Are those your logs under the stairs?" one of them
asked.

"Those are my logs," I said. "But they are not under the stairs. They are by a stone wall near the stairs."

"That makes no difference. It's a fire hazard and someone has filed a complaint. Get the logs out by tomorrow or we'll close you up."

I remembered my landlord's visit a week earlier. He had commented that I had a good pile of logs which should make a warm fire. He twirled his cane and looked at me from cat-grey eyes, set in a flabby yellow face crushed in a thousand wrinkles. As he minced about on his tiny feet, encased in patent leather pumps, I expected any moment to see the walls part or the ceiling open for his exit. When he left in the normal way, wishing me good luck and great success, I was sure he doffed his black homburg to me. Almost sure.

Now I threw my resolutions to the wind and phoned him, determined to take the offensive at any cost.

"Why did you call those fire inspectors?" I demanded. "Couldn't you have told me if I was breaking an ordinance?"

The more my voice rose, the more he chuckled.

Not long afterward a fat, tobacco chewing sloven entered the shop and stood looking around carefully, swaying on the balls of his feet. I thought he might be a tout, lost on his way to a bookie.

"Where does this wire go?" he finally asked.

"Go?" I said. "Who cares?"

"Don't get snotty with me, buddy," he said. "I'm going to close you up. I'm the city electrical inspector and we've got a complaint that your wiring is a hazard to the building."

He continued to stand in the middle of the floor, his hands locked behind his back, swaying back and forth like the old Jews on High Holidays in the Synagogue.

When he had gone, I called my landlord and cried, "Listen, you are killing me with inspection. Wish me bad luck and bankruptcy and leave me alone!"

Of course I had to get an electrical contractor, whose workmen tore the shop to pieces, removed perfectly good wiring, and replaced it.

A week later a tall man in a Brooks Brothers suit and carrying an attaché case came to collect the bill for $375.00. His smugness was so overwhelming that I turned and walked away from him. As I moved along, inspecting my bookshelves, he followed closely behind. I could see myself walking down Rush Street, going to dinner, going home, with this persistent, immaculate young man silently in attendance. Suddenly, turning, I stepped squarely on his polished shoes.

Excusing myself, I said, "You know, the man to pay you for this work is my landlord. If the wiring was faulty between the walls, obviously I have nothing to do with it. I'll call him up. You can talk with him."

My landlord must have been surprised at my cheery voice. "I have an interesting gentleman here who wants to talk with you," I said. "He is a genius. The work he did for you in the installation of BX wires between the walls is something to be seen to be appreciated. You'll marvel at its beauty. Here he is."

I handed over the receiver. The storm of words coming from the other end nearly blew the young man off his feet. I couldn't contain my laughter. I lurched over to a wall, holding my guts and laughing till I cried. It was marvelous. Wonderful. I had reversed the tables at last.

Naturally, I paid the bill. My landlord had new electrical outlets, but our relations were different. He continued to take advantage of me, but not any longer under the guise of wishing me "good luck" or a "great success."

My landlord helped me. He taught me to be on guard. He taught me that it is, in fact, cold outside. He put me on trial — rather like K in Kafka's *The Trial*. I could not just go running for help when trouble came. I could no longer retreat into the fantasy of pretending that running a bookstore was not a business. He taught me that the world requires people to take abuse, lying, cheating, duplicity — and outlast them.

Now when my landlord came to visit me, it was on an entirely new emotional basis. Nothing was different in appearance, yet in feeling everything was changed because I was no longer afraid. When he cheated me now, it was only a cheap triumph for him. I was free because I had become inwardly secure. I did not beat the Devil, but I knew positively that the Devil exists, that evil is real. Let him do his worst — his absolute worst — so long as you can handle yourself, he cannot ultimately triumph. Where K failed in *The Trial* was in his emotional inability to handle his threatened ego.

K's trial is allegorical. So was my landlord. Only with the imagination can we see through into what is real. My landlord was one of the disguises of evil. I know now that had I let him throw me, I could never have withstood the trials of reality that were to come.

3

How to Get Started
in the Book Business

I HAD decided to become a bookseller because I loved
good books. I assumed there must be many others who
shared a love for reading and that I could minister to their
needs. I thought of this as a calling. It never occurred to
me to investigate bookselling as a business.

Had I done so, I should have learned that eighty percent of all the hardcover books purchased across the counter in America are sold by twenty booksellers. If I had
been given the facts and sat down with pencil and paper,
I could have discovered that to earn a living and continue
to build the kind of inventory that would make it possible
to go on selling, I would need to have an annual gross in
the neighborhood of $100,000!

Even if I had had the facts in hand, they would
not have deterred me. If vows of poverty were necessary,
I was ready to take them. And I refused to be distressed
by the expressions on people's faces when I confided that
I was about to make a living selling books. Sell freight,

yes. Sell bonds or stocks or insurance, certainly. Sell pots
and pans. But books!

And I was not only going to sell books — I was going to
sell *real* books: those that dealt seriously and truly with
the spirit of man.

I had finished cleaning and decorating my little shop
before it dawned on me that I did not know how to go
about the next step: getting a stock of books and records
to sell. A study of the classified telephone directory revealed the names of very few publishers that sounded at
all familiar. Was it possible there were no publishers in
Chicago? If that were the case, would I have to go
to New York?

There was a telephone listing for Little, Brown and
Company, so I called them. The lady there said she would
be glad to see me. She proved to be very kind and very
disillusioning.

"No," she said, "the book business is not easy, and your
location is bad. No, the big publishers will not sell to you
direct because your account is too small. No, we at Little,
Brown won't either. If I were you, I'd forget the whole
idea and go back to teaching."

Everything was No. But she did tell me where I could
buy books of all publishers wholesale, and that was the information I wanted. I hastened to A. C. McClurg's and
presented myself to the credit manager.

The fact that I had a shop, nicely decorated, did not
seem to qualify me for instant credit. First I would have
to fill out an application and await the results of an in-
vestigation. In the meantime if I wanted books, I could
buy them for cash.

"All right," I said. "I want to buy three hundred dollars worth of books."

"That isn't very much," the man said. "How big is your store?"

"Well," I said, "it's fifteen feet long and nine feet wide, and I'm going to carry records, too."

He shook his head and, with a sidewise glance, asked, "What did you say your name was?" Then, still apparently somewhat shattered, he directed me to a salesman.

I launched into my buying terribly, terribly happy, yet filled with all sorts of misgivings. Was I selecting the right books? And who would I sell them to? But I had only to touch their brand new shiny jackets to restore my confidence. I remember buying Jules Romain's *Men of Good Will*. In fifteen years, I never sold a copy. I'm still trying. I bought Knut Hamsun, Thomas Mann, Sigrid Undset, Joseph Hergesheimer, Willa Cather, Henry James — as much good reading as I could obtain for $298.49. I was promised delivery as soon as the check cleared.

When the books arrived on a Saturday morning, it was like a first love affair. I waited breathlessly as the truck drew up, full of books for my shop. It wasn't full at all, of course — not for me, anyway. My books were contained in a few modest boxes. And I had built shelves all the way up to the ceiling!

Again, a moment of panic. Enough, my heart said. Stay in the dream! What's next?

The next step was to get recordings. In this field, at least, I found that all the major companies had branch offices in Chicago. I called Columbia records and was told they'd send me a salesman.

He arrived a few days later, blue eyed and blond haired, an interesting man with a sad message. "No, we can't open you up," he said. "It's out of the question. Your store is in direct conflict with Lyon and Healy on the Avenue. So there's no question about it, we can't give you a franchise. We won't. Decca won't. And I'm sure RCA won't."

I was overcome with rage. Didn't he know I had fought to keep this country free? Wasn't there such a thing as free enterprise? Didn't I have a right to compete in a decent and honorable manner? If I couldn't get records one way, I'd get them another, I assured him. Strangely enough, he seemed to like my reaction. Later he was able to help me.

But for the present, I was reduced to borrowing more money from my brother-in-law with which to buy off-beat recordings from an independent distributor. I brought my own phonograph from home and my typewriter and settled down to the long wait for the first customer.

How do you get going in a business of which you have no practical knowledge and which inherently is a doomed undertaking to begin with? The only answer is that you must be favored with guardian angels.

The first one to bring a flutter of hope into my life came into it on a September afternoon at a luncheon affair, under I do not know what auspices, for Chicago authors. There I encountered a distinguished looking white-haired gentleman, tall but with the sloping back of a literary man, standing mildly in a corner. I introduced myself to Vincent Starrett, bibliophile and Sherlock Holmes scholar.

He listened attentively to my account of myself and took my phone number. A few days later he called to ask for more information about my idea of combining the sale of books and records.

I pointed out that it was easy, for example, to sell a copy of Ibsen's *Peer Gynt* if the customer was familiar with Grieg's incidental music for the play. Besides, reading and listening were closely allied activities. Anyone with literary tastes could or should have equivalent tastes in music. It was logical to sell a record at the same time you sold a book. Mr. Starrett thought this was a fine idea, and to my shocked surprise, wrote a paragraph about me in his column in the Book Section of the *Chicago Sunday Tribune*.

The Monday after the write-up appeared, I could hardly wait to get to the shop. I expected it would be flooded with people. It wasn't. The phone didn't even ring. I was disappointed, but still felt that hidden forces were working in the direction of my success. Mr. Starrett's kind words were a turning point for me — I no longer felt anonymous.

Some people did see the write-up — intelligent, charming, good people, such as I had imagined gathering in my tiny premises. Among them were two young women who were commercial artists. One day they complained that there was nothing in the store to sit on, and after I had stumbled for excuses, they presented me with a bench decorated on either side with the inscriptions: "Words and Music by Stuart Brent," and "Time Is Well Spent with Stuart Brent." Now I felt sure things were looking up.

My next good genie and an important influence in my life was a short, bald gentleman with horn-rimmed spectacles who stood uncertainly in the doorway and asked, "Where's the shop?"

He was Ben Kartman, then Associate Editor of *Coronet Magazine*, a man as kind and thoughtful as he is witty and urbane. He came in and looked around, studied the empty shelves, and shook his head. He shook his head often that afternoon. He wondered if I was seriously trying to be a bookseller — or was I just a dreamer with a hideout?

Surely I wanted to survive, didn't I? Surely I wanted to sell books. Well, in that case, he assured me, I was going about it all wrong. For one thing, I had no sign. For another, I had no books in the windows. And most important of all, I had no stock. How can you do business without inventory? You can't sell apples out of an empty barrel.

I took all his comments without a sound.

Then Ben said, "Sunday come out to the house. I've got a lot of review copies as well as old but saleable books. Even if you don't sell them, put them on the shelves. The store will look more prosperous."

He gave me several hundred books from his library, which we hauled to the store in his car. The Seven Stairs began to look like a real bookshop.

Ben Kartman also decided that I needed publicity. Not long afterward, my name appeared in a daily gossip column in one of the Chicago newspapers. Ben said that these daily puffers could be important to me, and this proved to be the case.

Meshing with my association with Kartman was another significant influence — a man who certainly altered my life and might have changed it still more had he lived. He was Ric Riccardo, owner of a famous restaurant a quarter of a mile down the street from my shop, and one of the most extraordinary and magnetic personalities I have ever encountered. He was an accomplished artist, but it was his fire, his avid love of life, his utterly unfettered speech and manner, his infatuation both with physical being and ideas that drew the famous and the somewhat famous and the plain hangers-on constantly to his presence. He is the only great romantic character I have known.

He first came into my store one day before Christmas. He wore a Cossack fur hat and a coat with a huge mink collar and held a pair of Great Danes on a leash. He had the physique of Ezio Pinza and the profile (not to mention more than a hint of the bags beneath the eyes) of his friend, the late John Barrymore. He was tremendous. He told me all he wanted was some light reading to get his mind off his troubles.

Later when Riccardo and the Danes entered the shop, virtually filling it, I would stand on a chair to converse with him. He was very tall and it gave me a better chance to observe him. Although his language was often coarse, he shunned small talk or fake expressions. The only time he ever reprimanded me was the day I used the phrase, "I've got news for you." As our friendship became firm, I would often join him after closing the store for a bowl of green noodles (still a great specialty of the restaurant which is now managed by his son).

Now if, as Ben said, I did everything wrong, there was

at least one thing I certainly did not neglect to do. I talked to people. I knew my books and I knew what I was talking about. Ideas were and are living things to me and objects of total enthusiasm. It hurt me terribly if someone came in and asked for a book without letting me talk with him about it. The whole joy of selling a book was in talking about the ideas in it. It was a matter of sharing my life and my thought and my very blood stream with others. *That* was why I had been impelled into this mad venture — unrelated to any practical consideration beyond enthusiasm for the only things that seemed to me to be meaningful. Ric was one of those who responded to this enthusiasm.

One very cold February morning, a cab stopped outside the shop. I saw two men and a woman get out and come up the stairs. There was a good fire going in the fireplace and it was quiet and warm inside.

Ric was the only member of the trio I recognized, although the other man looked at me as though I should know him. But the woman! She wore the longest, most magnificent mink coat I had ever seen, the collar partially turned up about her head. When she spoke, I backed away, but she stepped in and extended her hand to me. It was Katharine Hepburn.

"Oh, yes, that's Katie," the unidentified man said, and all of them laughed at my obvious confusion. Miss Hepburn sat on my decorated bench and held out her hands to the fire.

Ric said, "Stuart, my boy, this is Luther Adler."

I was too nervous to say anything as we shook hands.

I could only keep staring at Katharine Hepburn. I adored her. I loved her accent and those cheekbones and that highly charged voice. I wanted so much to do something for her but I couldn't think of anything to do.

Suddenly Ric said, "Let's buy some books."

Mr. Adler looked about and said, "Do you have a book for a Lost Woman?"

I said, "Yes," and handed him a copy of Ferdinand Lundberg's new book, *Modern Woman: The Lost Sex*. He gave it to Miss Hepburn, saying, "Here, Katie, this is for you."

Without a pause, she turned and said, "Do you have a good book for a Lost Jew?"

"Yes," I said, and produced a Sholem Asch volume.

She gave it to Mr. Adler, saying, "Here, Luther, this is for you."

They bought many books that morning, and I was swept away in wonder and exhilaration at the possibility of bringing happiness to Lost Women, Lost Jews, the Beautiful and the Great, alike in their needs with all of us for the strength and joy of the spirit. It was wonderful — but it was awful when I had to take their money.

A world very much like that of my dreams began to open up. People came. Authors began to congregate around the fireplace. The shop was visited by newspaper writers like Martha King, of the *Chicago Sun-Times*, who wrote a charming article, for which I was deeply grateful. I was beginning to do business, although still without a cash register. The rent was paid promptly, and McClurg's permitted me to have a charge account. One or two Eastern publishers even let me have some books on open account. And the man from Columbia Records kept dropping by, leading me to believe that they might be thinking about me in spite of their presumed obligations to Lyon and Healy.

Why did people come, often far out of their way and at considerable inconvenience? I was too busy to reflect upon the matter at the time. There was nothing there but the books and me — and a great deal of talk. But some need must have been filled — by moving people to take notice of themselves, forcing them to think about what they were reading or what they were listening to. We talked a lot of small talk, too, but it was small talk with heart in it. And the effect was contagious. Those who came told others and they came too.

The place acquired a life of its own, which will be the subject of many of the following pages. But that life, real and wonderful as it was, could not endure. Perhaps it is worth writing about because it is *not* a success story — and what came after has its meaning in the reflected tenderness and flickering hope those years taught one to cherish.

This is not merely a sentimental record. It has no point unless seen against the background of the cultural poverty of our society — and the apparent economic impossibility of alleviating that poverty through commercial channels such as the publication and distribution of books.

The plain fact is, the kind of business I wanted to immerse myself in does not exist. One of the reasons it does not exist is because the publishing industry does not —

and quite possibly cannot — support it, even to the extent of supplying its reason for being: good books. The business of publishing and the profession of letters have become worlds apart. The arts are being bereft of their purpose through a horrifying operation known as "the communications industry," an industry geared for junk eaters.

Publishing is "bigger" and more profitable today than ever before, largely because of the mushrooming of educational institutions and the consequent demand for textbooks. Wall Street has gone into publishing; there is money in it. But the money is in mass distribution — through the schools, through the book clubs. It is little wonder that the individual, personal bookseller is an anachronism, lost sight of by the publishers themselves. The bookseller may feel outraged, as I did, when a publisher sells him books, then sends out a mailing piece to the bookseller's customers offering the same books at a much lower price. The practice is certainly unfair, but the bookseller has become a completely vestigial distributing organ. What the publisher is really looking forward to is the possibility that one of the book clubs will take some of his publications, further slashing the price beyond the possibility of retail competition.

And what of the writer? If he can turn out bestsellers, he can live like a potentate. But the sure-fire formula in this field is to pander to a sex-starved culture and a dirty, vulgar one to boot. A book written by this or any other formula can't be worth anything. A true book must be part of the individual's life and spirit.

It is commonplace to blame the public for what the public gets. And no doubt the public must take the blame. But I am not interested in giving the public what it wants if this means corrupting man's spirit even through as ineffectual a medium as the printed word.

As a matter of fact, I have never had what people wanted to read ("Your competitor just bought fifty copies of this title," the publisher's representative would tell me, shaking his head hopelessly), and I lost out because of it. But my personal satisfaction derived from recommending some book, possibly an old one, that I thought would bring the reader something fresh and real.

Anything that touches the heart or stirs the mind has become a matter for apology. I think of Mary Martin coming out on the stage in *South Pacific* and begging the audience's indulgence and forgiveness for having to admit to them that she was in love with a wonderful guy!

Is it any wonder that modern men and women are so threatened, frightened, and weak when they have lost the capacity for love, tenderness, and awe — capacities which should be nourished by what we read? And especially the men. "Where are the men?" the women ask. Once a man has joined "the organization," the love of a real woman offers a basic threat. The organization man doesn't want to be challenged by a relationship any more than by an idea.

It was to these deficiencies in people's lives that I had hoped to minister. Reading remains a positive leverage to keep us from becoming dehumanized. But easy reading won't do it, or phony Great Book courses that foster smugness and an assumed superiority (read the ads purveying this kind of intellectual snobbery).

We can't go on devaluating the human spirit and expect some miracle to save us. Even Moses couldn't get the Red Sea to divide until a stranger acted upon absolute faith and jumped in. I felt my job was to get people to jump — to read something, old or new, that could engage them in some real vision of human possibilities: to read Albert Camus or Graham Greene or Rollo May or Erich Fromm. To read again (or for the first time) Ibsen's *Peer Gynt* or Kafka's *The Trial*, Bruno Bettelheim's *The Informed Heart*, F. S. C. Northrop's *Philosophical Anthropology*, or Father duChardin's *The Phenomena of Man*.

I decided I could sell a good book just as easily as a bad book. In the days following the visit of Katharine Hepburn, I placed *Modern Woman: The Lost Sex* into the hands of many women, and the responses were gratifying and illuminating. Finally I wrote a letter to Ferdinand Lundberg, co-author of the book, telling him of one of the most interesting of these incidents. He sent the letter along to Mary Griffiths, then advertising manager for Harper and Brothers, who asked permission to reprint it in its entirety as an ad in the *Chicago Tribune* book section. A phenomenal sale resulted. I sold hundreds of copies and so did other Chicago booksellers.

It looked as though things were opening up for me, as though I might be on the way toward proving my point. And perhaps something was proved. Much later when in a state of great depression I wrote a gloomy letter to Hardwick Moseley, sales manager of Houghton Mifflin, he responded by saying, "Never will I permit you to leave the book business. If we had fifty more like you in the United States we might have a business!" But for so many reasons, some of which I have just dwelt on, the odds against fifty such enterprises flowering — or any of them flourishing — are very, very great.

Meantime, however, several colorful years of the Seven Stairs lay ahead, and, beyond that, an unimagined range of encounter in the diverse realms of art and letters, psychiatry, commerce, and, that monster of the age, television.

4

Building the Seven Stairs

You'd be surprised how humiliating it can be to wrap books in cramped quarters.

As business grew, Saturday afternoon became a great but soul-shattering time for me. The shop was filled with people, music, conversation. There was the delicious thrill of selling, tarnished still by the dubious proposition of taking money, and followed finally by the utter physical subjugation of package wrapping. One moment I was riding a wave of spiritual exhilaration; the next moment I was the contorted victim of some degrading seizure as I grappled with paper and twine while people pressed about me. The shop was too small!

Ben Kartman had constantly encouraged me to expand. But expand where? Well, there was a back room occupied by a dancer who had given up his career because of a psychotic fear of travel. It was a fine, big room, and it too had a fireplace. He was very friendly and I had helped him find a bit of solace through Havelock

Ellis' *The Dance of Life*. The only course now seemed to
be to persuade him to move into one of the vacant studios
upstairs. This proved not difficult to do so far as he was
concerned, but what of our landlord?

So again I was calling my landlord, and with his voice
dripping with its usual sweetness he invited me to come
right over.

It was all just the same, the little patent leather shoes,
the pin striped trousers, the pearl grey vest, the stickpin
in the tie, the waxed moustache, the mincing steps across
the thick rugs of the rich, imperious, and somewhat de-
cayed quarters. There was the same circuitous conversation with a thousand extraneous asides, but somehow it
resulted in my signing a two-year lease for the doubled
space. And this time I didn't even need a co-signer. My
landlord felt sure my success was as good as made.

I firmly believed I was on my way, too. I had suffered and nearly broken more than once, but the dream
was working. I was building a store with love in it.
I wasn't merely selling books — I was teaching. And in
my awesome love for books, every package of fresh, new
volumes, cold and virginal to the touch, shining with invitation, returned my devotion with a sensuous thrill. In
discovering this world, I felt I had discovered myself. I
had been tested, and the future was open before me.

Of course, I had no money. But I was young, my nervous system could take endless punishment, my stomach
could digest anything, and I could sleep on a rock. Be-
holden to no one, I hit upon a principle: If an idea is psy-
chologically sound, it must be economically feasible.

Now I was sure. The breakthrough was more than the penetration of a wall into another room. It would be a breakthrough for my heart and a new beginning in my life.

The first thing to do was to bring in a building contractor. He surveyed the situation and assured me that the job was simple — two men could do it in a week. It would cost about one thousand dollars.

Well what about it? Of course all of my profits were tied up in increased stock, but I was certainly not going to let money check my enthusiasm at this point. The time had come, I decided, to see about a bank. Every day while riding the bus I saw signs offering me money on my signature only. Do you want a new car? Need to pay old bills? Buy a car? Buy a refrigerator? Buy anything? See your friendly banker. What really decent fellows these bankers must be!

I had also been told at the separation center that as a former soldier I was entitled to certain kinds of help from a grateful government, which included financial backing in any promising business venture. I could not see anything standing seriously in the way of my borrowing a thousand dollars for my breakthrough.

Therefore, bright and early on a fine morning, I went to the bank. I had dressed myself with care. My tie was straight and my shirt clean. I wore my only suit. My shoes were shined. I had shaved carefully and brushed my hair with purpose. After all, I reasoned, a banker is a banker — you must respect him. I had never known a banker before in my life, and I scare easily.

When I sat down with the bank officer, I was glad I had taken care to make a good impression, for he looked me over while I stated my business. Apparently his mind was not on my attire, however.

"Do you carry life insurance?" he said.

"No, sir."

"Do you have a car?"

"No, sir."

"Do you have stocks or bonds?"

I felt slightly ill. No one in my entire life had ever mentioned stocks or bonds to me.

"Then what will you do for collateral?"

Again a word no one had ever used in front of me.

I tried another tack. "I believe I ought to tell you more about myself." Then my voice dried up. Tell him what? That when I was in college, I learned the *Ode to the West Wind* by heart? That I believed in the impossible? That I would rather die than fail to meet an obligation to his bank? It would never do . . . not for this man with the pale, hard eyes.

He was not unkind to me. He pointed to a little, old lady across the floor and said, "Now suppose that woman making a deposit were told that I made a loan to you of one thousand dollars without the security of any collateral, do you know what she could do? She could have me fired for jeopardizing her savings."

I didn't have the heart to ask about the happy signs in the buses, but grasped at one last straw. "Isn't it a fact," I said, "that the government will guarantee this kind of loan if I can show justification for it?"

He admitted this was correct. "But we'd rather not make that kind of loan," he said.

That was twelve years ago. Today the banks are generous and I can get a loan without shining my shoes or straightening my tie. The answer is terribly simple. Banks only loan money to those who already have it.

I walked defeated along Michigan Avenue under the cloudless sky. It was all so simple, logical, and perfectly mechanical. I just couldn't make something out of nothing, no matter how strong my will or how deep my faith. I had to have money.

As I walked, a comment of my father's flitted through my mind: "Some men make it early in life, but you, my son, will make it a little late in life. But you'll make it." I said to myself, "Look, nothing has changed. Nothing at all. If you don't expand, what of it? Are you beginning to think of the kind of success that feeds the infantile longings of so many adults? What's wrong with what you've accomplished?"

I remembered going to my father to talk about college. "Go to college," he told me. "It is very important to get a college education. I'm right behind you."

"It takes money to go to college," I said.

"Money?" he said. "What fool can't go to college with money? The idea is to make it without money!"

And so I did.

I was feeling better when I reached the shop, but was still so deep in my soliloquy that I rested my head on the desk and did not even hear Ben Kartman's steps when he came up the stairs.

"What's the trouble, Stuart?" he said, standing in the doorway looking at me.

"I went to the bank," I told him. "They turned me down. I'm a poor credit risk and they never heard of World War II, believe me. So there'll be no expansion."

"How much will the construction cost?"

"A thousand dollars."

"But you'll need some more money for stock and to fix the place up, won't you?"

"I guess so."

"Well?" He began to laugh while I talked my problem out. Finally he stopped laughing and I stopped talking.

"Get your hat and come with me," he said. "I'll get you the money."

We went to the bank together. Ben signed the notes with his house as collateral. I got the money and the breakthrough began. But I owed the bank two thousand dollars! I no longer slept so well.

Anyway, down went the partition and the Seven Stairs expanded. Joe Reiner, then sales representative for Crown Publishers, happened in and, observing that I needed more book shelving, took me to see Dorothy Gottlieb, who was moving her Gold Coast book store to the Ambassador East Hotel. She had plenty of shelving to sell.

On a Sunday morning, Joe and I got a mover to bring in the new fixtures. We came puffing and grunting in with the shelving and nearly annihilated my sick ballet dancer, who was supposed to have moved out a week before. He lay on a mattress in the middle of the floor and, upon seeing us, let out a yell and drew the blankets up to his chin, crying, "What do you think this is? A Frank Capra movie? Here I lie on my virtuous couch, too ill to move, and you . . . !"

I developed several successful techniques for selling books. For example, when I read a book that I liked very much, I would send out a post card to everyone I believed might be interested in it also. There is not much room on a post card, so the words describing the value of the book had to be selected carefully. I avoided the dust jacket phrases. "Great," "brilliant," and "exciting" won't cut any mustard. You must know your book and know your mailing list.

Another technique was the use of the phone call — a very delicate tool that must not be employed indiscriminately. The call must, first of all, be made to someone who you are reasonably sure won't resent it. And you must know exactly what to say and say it quickly.

When a friend came into the store, I might greet him with "Ah, guter brudder, glad you stopped in. I have a book for you." Or, "Here is a new Mozart recording you must hear."

To have a successful book store means also to be a slave to detail. This I found killing. Often I would struggle for hours to track down a title someone had requested, go to the trouble of ordering it (more often than not on a money in advance basis), only to find that the customer no longer wanted the book. Or I would special order a book, run like a demented fool over to the customer's office to deliver it personally, and discover that the wrong book had been ordered in the first place. You could pretend to yourself that this kind of service would endear you to the customer and cement a faithful relationship, but it didn't always work that way.

I worked hard, but my customer relations were not always perfect. I demanded that customers buy books for the same reasons that I sold them — out of a serious regard for greatness. I could not stand having myself or my books and records treated as a toy by the jaded and self-satisfied. And I was a jealous god. Today I know better, yet I instinctively back away from a customer who comes into the store carrying a package from another bookseller.

But well or poorly done, it took all kinds of doing: typing post cards, making phone calls, washing and sweeping the floor, cleaning the windows and shelves, running to the post office, delivering books, and talking in the meanwhile on the mind of Spinoza, the beauty of the Mozart D Minor Quartet, the narrative power of Hemingway, or the value of *The Caine Mutiny*, which on first appearance was slow to catch on.

Still, the business was developing. Each day I met someone new. Each day presented new challenges to one's strength and intuition and pure capacity for survival. Around this struggle there developed a convivial circle which was ample reward for anything. On any Saturday afternoon it might include Nelson Algren, Jack Conroy, Studs Terkel, Ira Blitzsten, Dr. Harvey Lewis,

Marvin Spira, Evelyn Mayer, David Brooks, and Dr. Robert Kohrman, holding forth on an inexhaustible range of subjects, filling the air with tobacco smoke, drinking fiercely strong coffee from sometimes dirty cups, and munching salami and apples. The world of the Seven Stairs was beginning to form.

For months I practically made a career of selling Nelson Algren's neglected volume of short stories, *The Neon Wilderness*. Nelson had already received considerable acclaim for the book, as well as his already published novels, *Somebody in Boots* and *Never Come Morning*, but short stories don't sell (it is said). In any event, these stories represent some of Algren's finest work (which at its best is very fine indeed), and I placed the book in the hands of everyone who came into the shop. I sold hundreds of copies. Then to keep the book alive, we held periodic parties. One month we would call it Nelson's birthday, another month the birthday of the publication of the book, still another the birthday of the book itself. We invariably invited many of the same people, along with new prospects. At one point, Ira Blitzsten was moved to remark that he didn't want Nelson to autograph his copy as he wanted the distinction of being the only person in Chicago with an unsigned copy.

Algren is a tall, lanky individual with mussed blond hair and a sensitive face, sometimes tight and drawn, some times relaxed. In those days he wore steel rimmed spectacles and Clark Street clothes — a pin stripe suit, a garish shirt, a ridiculous tie, in spite of which he still had a fairly conservative bearing. Once he even wore a bow tie that lit up.

He is a quiet man. You sense he has a temper, but he seldom uses it. He is an authority on the argot of the "wild side of the street," and I never heard him utter a vulgar word. He has the faculty of putting others at ease. When he talks with you, he gives you a remarkable singleness of attention. Even if the room is overflowing with people, you know that he is listening only to you.

He is a loner who reveals nothing of his private life. In fact, he never gave me his address. When he is introduced to someone, he shakes hands and nods his head at the same time. He gives you the simultaneous impression of understanding and remoteness. You are not surprised to find that his humor is sardonic.

Nelson Algren and Jack Conroy could perform a remarkable duet on the subject of James T. Farrell, Conroy in a broad Irish accent, Algren in a clipped, half muttering manner. I never learned the personal source of their animosity, but the name of Farrell had the magic to channel all their hostilities and frustrations into a fountain of pure malice. It was wonderful.

Sometimes Nelson brought his mother. Sometimes he would bring with him one of the girls related to the novel he was then writing, *The Man with the Golden Arm*. One night Nelson took me to "the wild side." We entered a Clark Street tavern, a long, bare hall perhaps 150 feet long and thirty feet wide. Along one wall stretched a huge bar. It was a busy evening — every stool was occupied. We crossed the wooden floor to the other side of the room where there were rows of small tables with folding chairs set around them. Before we were seated, one of the men at the bar slugged his woman in the mouth, and the two fell off their stools, blood gushing, and landed, one on top of the other on the floor. The bartenders came around and dragged them out, pitching them into the street.

A moment later one of the bartenders was at our table asking for our order. He knew Nelson, and they chatted easily. I was, frankly, sniffing, for as the stale beer smell of the place settled, I had a sense of being literally in a zoo.

As I looked about, I observed a mesh of wire fencing across the section of the ceiling beneath which we were sitting. I got up and inspected. There above us were live monkeys sitting on a bar behind the fence. I sat down and asked Nelson what this meant.

He said, "Wait and see."

The tavern din was terrible, a demonic blend of shouting, laughing, swearing, name-calling — the human cries at inhuman pitch. It was out of a Gorky novel.

We drank several beers and waited, talking very little. Nelson's face seemed fixed in a slight smile of playful disdain. It was impossible to say of what.

My bafflement was intensified when two men walked in and approached the place where we were sitting. They pulled a ladder from the wall, climbed the steps, and opened the door of one of the cages. One of the men took a monkey by the leather strap attached to its collar, placed it on his back, and climbed down the ladder. He walked to the far end of the room, opened a door, went in, and closed the door after him and his companion.

I sat rooted to my seat, failing to understand what I had seen. Was this in some way the meaning behind the phrase, "a monkey on his back"? I knew that whatever was going on here could scarcely be an idle zoological experiment, yet somehow I felt an impenetrable wall between my innocence and the full possibilities of human depravity.

I looked once more at the people in the tavern, and all at once it was with different eyes. I no longer saw them as "dregs" and "strays." I saw something terrible, humiliating, too outrageous to form into words.

What is happening? Who are these people? Are they, indeed, people? But am I? Have I an identity?

My smugness melted and the distaste I had felt for what I saw now angered me. I had come into this place small, mean, and superior, a cad and a fop, the epitome of what I had long viewed with scorn in others.

I had a better notion of what Nelson was seeing and the nature of his protest. He had shown me a world where people lived without choice or destination.

I lived for days with this nightmare, asking myself why I should feel guilt for those who no longer feel responsible for themselves. Then it occurred to me that the question was never one of guilt, but only of love. The agony exists regardless of the setting. The lack of love is not alone on Clark Street.

To be successful, an autographing cocktail party must be planned with consummate skill and attention to detail.

You must leave nothing to chance. You may not pretend that everything will work out satisfactorily at the last minute. It will not. And because I respected writers so much, I tried to guard them against the ultimate humiliation of sitting at a table before a pile of their own books, with no buyers.

I adopted the following procedure: First, get from the author his own list of names — people he would like personally to invite to his party. Phone each of them, or at least write a post card asking if they are interested in receiving a signed copy of the book. Next, send out the invitation to all your charge accounts, then check the mailing list for people you think will be interested in the book. Avoid freeloaders. Invite the press and the literary critics and try to write a short human interest story for the columnists. In short, build up as big an advance as possible.

Furthermore, don't throw a skimpy party. People carry away impressions, and the only inpression you can afford is a bountiful one. It is said that all the world loves a lover, but one thing you can be sure of is that they love a winner. So avoid failure by planning against it, and then pray. Pray that it won't rain or turn freezing cold, that the pipes won't break or the electricity be turned off. Pray that you may fulfill your multiple responsibilities; to the author, the publisher, and your own hopes for continuing operation.

It seemed natural that one of our greatest cocktail parties should be given for Nelson Algren upon publication of *The Man with the Golden Arm*. Yet behind the scenes things went very oddly, and for a time it was hard to tell whether either the author or the publisher wanted the party — or the large downtown department store, either, which entered the picture as a prospect for the event.

Anyway, it took place at the Seven Stairs. Ken McCormick, Editor-in-Chief of Doubleday, Nelson's publisher, flew into Chicago. I can see him still, loaded with books in both arms, carrying them from one room to another.

There was high excitement — newspaper photographers and an unbelievable crush of people. It all began to tell on Nelson's nerves and mine. It seemed to me he was writing too long in each book, and at times he would change his mind in the middle of an inscription and ask for another copy (to Nelson such revision was a literary exercise, to me a spoiled copy was a financial loss). The line of guests seemed endless and I began to develop an active dislike for people, for money, for the whole business. Besides, it was getting awfully hot. Nelson and Ken and I removed our coats. Nelson even gave up writing long paragraphs in each book. I tried keeping a cool drink at his side at all times. It seemed to help.

It was a great but strange party. Nelson was a success, and in a way I was, too. And this altered things enormously. It had never occurred to me how people attach themselves to the rescue phantasy, how easily failure inspires love, how differently even the semblance of success affects relationships. All at once, people who had only wanted to help me became hypersensitive and found me snubbing them. And I was feeling a new sensitivity also: "You can't destroy me in the process of buying from me." It was the beginning of a new struggle.

The last guest finally left. Ken McCormick was a very happy publisher. I swept all interior confusions aside and counted up the books. We had sold one thousand copies of *The Man with the Golden Arm* in a single night! It was almost too much for Ken — he had to see it to believe it. And we were all dead tired. Just as I was about to turn the last light switch before we went out the door, I remembered and asked Nelson to autograph a book for me. As he bent down to write, I could see Bob Kohrman and myself sitting on the sand dunes reading the galleys of the book. I remembered conversations with Nelson and Jack Conroy in regard to the title, and Jack's needling of Nelson when the advances were running out, saying, "Any day now you'll be begging to come to work on the encyclopedia" (the constant drudgery to which Jack has given most of his working hours for two decades.)

Nelson, crouching over the book, wrote: "For Stuart and Jennie. The best in the West (as well as the South, North and East). Because he's the boy with the golden wife — and she's the girl with the golden guy."

For there was indeed now a Jennie, a golden girl with whose short life mine was now linked in a more responsible relationship than I had ever imagined I would assume — a decisive part in the unimaginable future building before me.

We were all on our way now, but Jack Conroy was the last to leave. He had waited until the very end to say, "Papa, it was a fine party. I'm proud of you and your efforts for Nelson." They were all gone now, the columnists, the celebrities, the crowd that stretched in a file of twos almost to the corner drug store. Only Jack Conroy, a huge and gentle man with his "Hello, Papa," the extended hand, and the tiny stare in the blue, grey-flecked eyes, always waiting, wondering how you are going to accept his greeting.

This is the wild, humorous, tender man who gave Tennessee Williams his first important break, who first published Richard Wright, who wrote a best-seller thirty years ago that is highly regarded by the few who remember it, and who is rated as the second most popular American author in all of Russia, one below Melville and one above Poe.* His only material reward: a purported fortune in rubles which he has no intention of ever collecting.

When Jack edited *Midland Humor*, a discerning anthology published in 1947, he was late to his own party at the Seven Stairs. When he arrived, I was shaken, as I always am, by his look of, "Will I be scolded? Will I be forgiven?"

He can be the most jocular of men, and the most understanding. One afternoon over coffee at the Seven Stairs he reported at hilarious lengths on the drinking prowess of his friend, Burl Ives, who was then doubling between a cabaret engagement at the Blackstone Hotel and the vaudeville show at the Chicago Theater. I was in the depth of my psychiatric period and suggested that help might be in order.

* Conroy's works consist of two novels, *The Disinherited* and *A World to Win*, several children's books, and *They Seek the City*, a history of Negro migration written in collaboration with Arna Bontemps with the assistance of a Guggenheim Fellowship.

"He doesn't seem unhappy about it," said Jack, innocently.

Today Conroy, one of the most talented men in American letters, quietly stands and looks. When he talks, he stares directly at you, or turns his head entirely away and speaks to empty space.

I think he is the most honest man I have ever met: in his intent, in his appraisal of others and their writing, and in his own bereavement. As the gait grows slower, the shyness becomes more pronounced and the gaze extends away farther and farther.

He has been called the Samuel Johnson of the Chicago South Side. The designation fits in many ways — the large physical build, the forceful expression and comprehensive knowledge, the long toil in the compilation of reference works — and in some ways not at all. He has been many things, at times even a wandering player, and his physiognomy suggests a somewhat more cerebral William Bendix.

He can provide the most wonderful encouragement to others. But his own burden is lack of time — lack of time for all his obligations, for all he should do. Publisher after publisher offers him handsome advances, and he declines them. He knows he would not fulfill the obligation.

We were at lunch not long ago. "I'm going down to Mexico on my vacation," he said. "I'm going to visit Motley."

I had known the tragic eyes of Willard Motley, whose *Knock on Any Door* did not fill our friend, Algren, with any particular enthusiasm.

"You know, that Nelson is mean," Jack said. "He wrote

some nasty things about me in the *Reporter*. Did you see that?"

"No, I didn't."

"Well, he did. We used to see a lot of each other."

We walked back to the office building where Jack does his faithful, painstaking hack work.

"I'll drop you a line from Mexico," he said. "I'll tell Motley that you're writing a book. Take care of yourself. I'll see you when I get back."

The grey-blue eyes were suddenly swollen with sadness, and the voice stretched in a heavier drawl. I wished with all my heart that things would work out well for Jack Conroy.

The relationship between genius and disaster is too deep for me to comprehend. I do know that genius is never made; it is only discovered. There has to be a front runner. The notion that genius will out, regardless of circumstances, is simply to ignore the nature of genius, which must center upon itself in order to function. I sometimes think that the energy expended in creating a really imaginative work drains the humanity out of the artist. If his personal life suffers as a consequence, his business acumen is even more incidental.

The Man with the Golden Arm was Algren's great commercial success, and the harvest was reaped by others. The story is told, or at any rate that part which has any bearing on this discourse, in a classic letter from Nelson to Otto Preminger, producer of the movie which bore the title, if not the imprint, of the novel:

Hotel Vermillion
6162 West Hollywood Blvd.
Los Angeles, California
February 16, 1955

Mr. Otto Preminger
Columbia Studios
1438 Gower Street
Los Angeles, California

Dear Mr. Preminger:

I am advised by your office that arrangements are now under
way to award me the sum of two hundred and three dollars
and seventy-eight cents, spent by myself to proceed, upon your
invitation, to the city of Los Angeles. I find this gesture most
generous, but am compelled to inform you that this money was
spent to no purpose to which you are member. Thank you all
the same.

I am further instructed that arrangements are also under way
to compensate me, at the rate of thirty-five dollars per diem,
for listening to the expression of certain thoughts, after a
manner of speaking, by yourself. These occurred between
January 27th and 31st inclusively. But since these were all,
like the novel about which you wove them, the property of
other persons living or dead, I cannot in conscience honor
them by acceptance of such compensation. Again I am grateful.
And again I am instructed that a check for the sum of seven
hundred and fifty dollars, in addition to the above items, is due
me from yourself. I assume this may well be an effort to repay
me for some twelve pages of double-spaced typing I achieved
in an effort to discover what in God's name you were talking
about. Since these pages served only to confuse you further,
no moneys are rightfully due me. Yet your thoughtfulness
does not cease to move me.

Should this concern for me derive from a simple and heartfelt gratitude for a diversion afforded you for a full week by "an interesting person," as you so happily put it when the moment came for parting, I do not feel you are so much indebted. Although I did not find in you an interesting person, I did discover one of arrogance approaching the uncanny. Upon the basis of mutual amusement, therefore, I am the debtor. And since you are decidedly more uncanny than I am interesting, I must at a rough estimate, owe you close to forty dollars.

And forward this sum confident of your satisfaction in alms from any quarter, however small, and remain

your obedient servant
Nelson Algren

"He jests at scars who never felt a wound."

5

The Day My Accountant Cried

I DISLIKE being interrupted when I am interesting someone in a book. One late afternoon while I was engaged
in making a sale, my accountant tiptoed over and stood
close to me. I moved away, but he came close again. I
frowned; generally that was enough to frighten him. But
not this time.

"I must speak with you," he said. "It's very important."

"Well, what is it?" I said.

His thin shoulders sagged and when he finally spoke,
his voice contributed to the general impression of a small,
furry animal in a trap. "You are bankrupt," he squeaked.

My accountant was a limp rag of a man with a lined,
ashen face and a bald head spotted with a few patches
of nondescript hair. The color of his eyes was an odd mix-
ture, neither grey nor brown, and he never met your
gaze, but looked down at your feet or to one side. He
wore a grey suit with a vest that had specially made
pockets to contain his pharmaceutical supplies, including

not only pill boxes and bottles, but his own spoon and a collapsible cup.

Although he was very neat, he bit his fingernails to the quick. Still, I found his hands fascinating when he added up columns of figures. His figure 8's and his 7's had a special quality about them, a precision bordering upon elegance.

He came into the store once a month, went over my bookkeeping, prepared the necessary forms for my signature, and left. Sometimes he would linger for just a few minutes looking at titles on the bookshelves. Then he would turn, shrug his shoulders, and depart.

When he looked up and informed me tragically, "You are bankrupt," the words were utterly meaningless to me. "Wait until I finish," I said, waving him aside, "then we'll talk." His distress was pitiful, yet I couldn't help laughing.

Talk we did. He showed me the stack of unpaid statements, then my bank balance, then the cost of my inventory. There was no doubt about it: I *was* bankrupt. Those pretty 8's and magnetic 7's proved it. The ledger sheets with the long red and blue lines and the numbers so small and so beautifully shaped within the spaces spoke the awful truth. But somehow this truth meant nothing to me, except strangely to remind me of a story told by my father about a man who lost a leg but ran on as though he still possessed two.

I looked at my accountant in silence. He sat next to me, his squeaky voice now still, his red-rimmed eyes peering at me and at the evidence lying before us on the desk,

along with a neat pile of Kleenex sheets, a spoon, and a
bottle of pink medicine. My accountant's adam's apple
began moving silently in his throat and as I observed this,
I placed my man as a literary character with whom I
was well familiar, the awful little man in *The Magic
Mountain* who mashed all his food together, bent his head
over it, and shoveled and pushed the mess into his mouth.
Again I began to laugh helplessly, and my accountant
kept saying, "Not funny, not funny, remember — you are
bankrupt."

"What do you suggest?" I finally asked.

"There is not much *to* suggest," he said. "The books
show bankruptcy. File for bankruptcy and call it a day."

"Just like that?" I said.

"The figures are correct," he said. "To me this means
you must go out of business."

"But what does it mean to me? I love this business and
want to remain in it. I've spent three years building it
and look at the progress I've made!"

"It can't be helped," he said. "Business is business.
Your publishers are not sentimental. When they send you
books, they want to be paid."

Of course I intended to pay, I assured him. But I
couldn't pay everyone all at once. And if I was serving
as an agent for their wares, couldn't some of them wait?
Or couldn't I go to the bank for another loan?

"Impossible," he said. "Furthermore, no one cares
about your good work or your bad work. Your problem is
that you haven't the money to meet your bills."

Strangely enough — immorally perhaps — it had never

occurred to me that this was my problem. Finally I said, "As a favor to me, could you pretend that you hadn't come here this evening? Could you forget this conversation? As I see it, nothing has changed whatsoever. So far, the only person threatening me with bankruptcy is yourself. It seems to me that if you will just stop talking about it, I am no longer bankrupt."

My accountant poured himself a cupful of pink medicine, smacked his lips, and burst into tears. He assured me that I was partially responsible for his ulcerated stomach. And he told me of his fate . . . the three times he had tried to pass the C.P.A. examinations . . . the scorn and derision to which he was subjected by fools like me . . . the plight of his wife and his children . . . and his simple allegiance to the truth of numbers.

I began to feel terribly guilty. What had I done to him by not breaking beneath the impact of his shocking pronouncement? "Please don't cry," I said. "Nothing is really changed, actually. I just don't believe in figures. I don't believe in bankruptcy. I still believe in people, in myself, in my work. Sometimes I wake up in the morning feeling joyous and sometimes I go to bed feeling wretched, but that's life. However, it is entirely my fault for making you cry. I meant to take you seriously, but I have a complete contempt for figures."

I brought him some water in his own antiseptic cup and told him the story of the Little Prince and the Fox and how the Fox made the Prince repeat: "Remember always — what is essential is invisible to the eye. It is the time you have wasted on your rose that makes her so important. Love means care and labor and respect. You are responsible for what you love."

I observed a different accountant sitting before me. In the course of my resistance to the destruction of my dream, I had apparently turned upon him in a way that was completely novel, neither scorning him nor using him, but speaking to him as a member of the human race.

"I've never done this before," he admitted, wiping his eyes. "But your attitude in the face of certain failure just broke me up. And here I am . . . owning two houses, a piece of a hotel, and some stocks and bonds . . . more money than you'll probably ever see. Yet I realize how very little I have . . . on the other side of the ledger."

I was astounded that he was not angry, found a copy of *The Little Prince* to give him, and as he left called, "You've forgotten your spoon and the medicine." He hesitated a moment, but did not turn back.

My accountant never again told me I was bankrupt. Several months passed before I next saw him, but since I continued to ignore the "figure" side of the business, his absence did not disturb me. Then one bright and lovely morning he came in wearing a fresh, newly pressed suit and . . . no vest!

"How marvelous!" I said.

"No vest, ever again," he assured me.

"What happened?" I asked.

"Well, you remember when I left? I still didn't believe you, but I read *The Little Prince* that evening. I used to think that facts and the gathering of facts were the only basis for living. But I realize now it is a much harder job.

It is easier to be hypochondriac . . . or a slave to the logic of the marketplace . . . or anything but one's self."

Does experience teach? Is it possible that a human being may be altered or set free through the written word? Are books important? Is it important to be a bookseller? Even though you are going broke? I had been turning like a worm in an apple for so long that it seemed a little more turning could scarcely hurt me.

One night I was awakened by the insistent ringing of the telephone.

"Can you come down to the restaurant at once, son?" It was Ric Riccardo's voice.

In less than an hour, I was seated in a booth with Ric, the late Henry Beaudeaux, then art critic for the *Chicago Daily News,* and Michael Seller, a psychoanalyst, with whose professional world I had just begun an acquaintance through interesting circumstances which I shall soon describe.

After I had sipped my coffee, Ric smiled thinly and said, "Mike, tell him."

"How would you like to go into the publishing business?" Mike said.

Then Ric took over. Chicago needed a publishing house, he argued. He was going to put up the money and establish the organization. But we would publish only Chicago talent regardless of their métier . . art, poetry, novels, whatever. He continued for perhaps an hour in this vein, dwelling upon the resources of talent which existed in the Chicago area and the absurdity

of depending on New York to "discover" it. Finally, I
wanted to know where I fitted in.

"I supply the money," Ric said. "You set up the office,
start the company going, get the writers. Tomorrow we'll
meet with my lawyer."

He didn't ask whether I liked the idea. He knew I was
crazy about it and would work day and night to see it
through.

"Have you a name for the firm?" I said.

"We'll call it the BrentR Press," Ric said solemnly. And
with enthusiastic handclasps over this peculiarly ranch
house designation, we parted.

Our first book was to be an art book titled, *Eleven Plus
Four,* principally to indicate the number of drawings to
be found in the book. The drawings by John Foote were
considerably more astounding than the title, and Sydney
J. Harris, columnist for the *Chicago Daily News,* wrote as
literate and perceptive an introduction as one is likely to
encounter.

Ric and I worked like a pair of furies on the project.
My association with the enterprise had a promotional
value that helped business at the store and I felt certain
that the way ahead lay open and that hard work was all
that was required.

When Ric gave me a check for $5,000 and said, "Go
to a bank and open an account." I headed straight out to
find the vice president of the bank where I had but a few
years earlier been turned down for a loan. He was gone,
but in his place I found a banker who was also a man.

Following this successful encounter, I rushed back to show Ric the receipted deposit slip. He laughed and took me up to his studio. He pointed to an army footlocker and said, "Open it."

I did, and the sight of its contents overwhelmed me. It was full of money — currency of every denomination.

"When you need money, come upstairs and help yourself," he said. "Only tell me afterwards."

I wondered what my accountant would think. Even after his reformation, this kind of profligacy must have been beyond his comprehension.

At first nobody talked about it. Ric had become ill and he could not be seen. When there were urgent decisions to make, I was told, "Make them yourself." But I was not sure of myself, I explained. The answer was the same. Ric was not to be disturbed under any circumstances.

Two months passed before I was permitted to go to the hospital to see him. He lay curled up in bed like a child, incredibly thin, the close-cropped hair completely grey, the skin waxen. I sat beside him for a long time before he unwound his body and looked at me.

"Go ahead and work, son," he said. "You can do everything. When I get better we'll talk about the book. If you need anything, go see Charley. I'll call you when I can."

I left feeling certain that I would never see Ric alive. I called Michael Seller and asked him to level with me. "It was his heart," Mike said. In his judgment, it was just a question of time.

I hung up feeling that my world was coming to an end.

If Ric was wounded, I was, too. If his survival was in doubt, I questioned my own. Every pattern I touched, no matter how vital, seemed to resolve itself into my own lostness.

But we were all wrong, doctors and friends alike. Ric came back strong. To be sure, the bags about the eyes were more pronounced, the skin hung a bit loosely about the face and neck. But one had only to look into the eyes to see that the fire was still there. Ric was all right, loving life, loving people, giving joy to all who came into his presence.

There was a new mark upon him, however, of increased gentleness. He spoke gently, moved gently, dressed gently, even ate gently. When we played chess, it was no longer with the same intensity. He would even interrupt the game to talk about the nature of God. He was becoming non-attached.

Finally the book came off the press. It was a beautiful job of production, and everyone whose name was known in Chicago seemed to have come to the autographing party in the spacious rooms above the restaurant. Ric sat at a table surveying the scene, and couldn't have cared less. He was gracious to everyone. He nodded his approval at all the checks I had received for advance orders. He seemed pleased with my enthusiasm for success. But something had gone out of him—at least so far as ardor for parties and promotion was concerned.

Ric died one week later, and with him many dreams, the BrentR Press among them.

6

The Man with the Golden Couch

I AM a great believer in the theory of "attractiveness." This theory is a way of describing a commonly experienced relationship between external events and what you feel in your heart. Something inside tells you that you are "ready," and then out of the world of events happenings begin to occur which seem exclusively yours. The conditions were there all the time, but your heart wasn't ready to accept them — hence the "attractiveness" in the world did not reveal itself. But when your heart is ready, whatever it is ready for will be fulfilled.

Perhaps the first step in this fulfillment was my marriage to Jennie, a girl with a strong, fine face and long brow, a generous soul, and a brilliant talent. In spite of the growing fame of the Seven Stairs, we faced a hard struggle for existence. New people were coming to buy books, mink coats mingling with hand-me-downs, but I made only grudging concessions to what many of them wished to buy. I refused to carry how-to-do-it books, occult books, books written and published by charlatans, books pandering to junk-eaters. I wouldn't even "special order" junk.

While I was limiting my practice to the least profitable aspects of the book business, Jennie's personal income as a staff pianist at a television station was cut off completely when the management eliminated most of the musicians from the payroll. So she came to help at the Seven Stairs.

Late one evening when I was alone in the store, an unlikely customer came in, walking with a slightly swaying motion and conveying a general attitude of, "You can't help me. I'm on an inspection tour. Stay away." An effort to engage him in conversation met with stiff resistance, so I retreated unhappily behind my desk. Finally my man came over to the desk with a small volume of Rilke's poetry and asked whether I carried charge accounts. When he saw me hesitate, he dipped into his pocket and paid in cash, stripping the single dollar bills from a sizeable bank roll, a demonstration which added further to my resentment of Ira Blitzsten.

With the exception of Ben Kartman, no one played a more decisive part in shaping the future of my business than Ira. In spite of the initial impression he made on me, and my obvious reaction, he continued to come into the store, and we became friends. He was an amazing reader with an excellent library of books and recordings, and he had an uncle, he told me, who was a lover of opera and might be persuaded to buy books and records from me.

One morning I received a phone call from the uncle,

Dr. Lionel Blitzsten, who asked if I had a recording of the Verdi Requiem with Pinza. It was a rich, full, commanding voice, and I was glad to be able to reply that I did. He suggested that I bring it over immediately.

Fortunately, he lived not far from the shop, but in a world of opulence such as I had never encountered. On arrival, I was sent by the maid to wait upstairs in the master bedroom. The room was fitted out like an 18th century drawing room. One wall was entirely covered with books. Later I discovered that because of illness, he did most of his entertaining here. I waited nervously, and noticing money lying on top of the dresser, retreated across the thick Turkish rug to the threshold and stayed there.

He came up the stairs quickly — a man in a hurry, I thought. But I was unprepared for his appearance, a kind of giant panda, very short and bald, with perhaps a few grey hairs straying about the temples, and wearing awesomely thick glasses (he had been going blind for years). His breathing was difficult (his lungs had a way of constantly filling up from his exertions) and I was later informed that his heart, too, was giving out. Platoons of doctors had struggled to keep him alive over the years.

What was really arresting (and somewhat terrifying) about this fat, puffing little man was the face. Above the glasses, the skull seemed all forehead; beneath, the clean-shaven skin was baby pink and the mouth shaped like a rosebud and just as red. That was it, the mouth . . . and when he spoke, the voice was musical, no longer deep, but rather high in pitch.

Our initial transaction was completed in a moment.

The Doctor looked at the records, asked the price, made his way to the dresser, gave me two ten dollar bills, thanked me, and vanished as quickly as he had appeared. I walked down the stairs and left quietly, but my heart was pounding.

It was several weeks before Dr. Blitzsten called again, very late in the evening. I recognized the sing-song quality characteristic of his speech as he asked for several books. I had all of them except the one he particularly wanted . . . he said he needed it to refresh himself with a certain passage.

"Well, never mind," he said, "I'll get the book elsewhere tomorrow. Would you mind awfully delivering the others tonight?"

Again the maid let me in and sent me to the bedroom. I waited in the doorway until the Doctor motioned me in and asked me to deposit the books on a small table beside the bed. He was sitting up in bed supported by a backrest, a blinking Buddha in white, blue-trimmed pajamas and covered with a thin, fine blanket. As I started to introduce myself, he waved his hand and began to talk.

So far as I knew, I had never before met a psychoanalyst, and I had the feeling that my every word and move would be subject to his scrutiny and probably found wanting. As I answered his questions carefully, politely, haltingly, I became increasingly jumpy and nervous. My words wouldn't come together as they usually did. I found myself making the most ridiculous errors, catching myself up only to discover that I was blushing. I was in the wrong place and I wanted to go home.

Somehow he was able eventually to put me at ease and I merely sat and listened. Even when he voiced opinions on Shakespeare which I felt certain were dead wrong, I said nothing. What was important was the stream of his language which was rapid, endless, scintillating, inexhaustibly alive. His charm and wit, his knowledge of literature, and his Voltairian cynicism thrilled me, while his pin-point knowledge of Hebrew and Yiddish left me helpless.

Finally I was dismissed. He thanked me again for having gone out of my way to deliver the books and told me to "special order" the particular volume he needed (a technical work of which I had never heard). He had decided to wait for it.

The following morning, I opened an account for Dr. Blitzsten, and I called Ira to thank him for this introduction to his remarkable uncle. I felt that something rather peculiar was happening, but I had no idea that it was to open up an entirely new phase in my business and in my personal experience.

The departure which was to make the difference between my financial success or failure in the book business was inaugurated upon my third visit to Dr. Blitzsten's residence. This time I was received in the downstairs study, where the Doctor sat behind a tremendous, brilliantly polished desk. He offered me a drink, which I declined, for I was still very shy in his presence. Then he launched quickly into the plan he had formulated.

"I understand," he said, "that you have recently married. I understand that you have a struggling business. I should like to offer a suggestion. Psychoanalysts have to get most of their books directly from the publishers or from dealers in England. Why don't you put in a good stock of such books? There will be immediate demand when I tell my colleagues of it. And I will do one more thing, also. I'll help you buy the right titles.

"Take these five books and compile the bibliographies from them. Then come and see me Sunday afternoon and I'll help you make your selection."

I accepted a drink now, amazed by this sudden, generous offer and the possibilities it opened to me. All I could do was to sit and look, with a heart too flooded with emotion for speech. I found words, finally, which must have been the proper words, for he smiled gently as he saw me to the door.

"Sunday afternoon, then. Goodnight," he called.

On Sunday morning the phone rang. It was Dr. Blitzsten telling me that I should bring Jennie too. On arrival, we were escorted into the living room. Again I felt in the presence of a world of unbelievable grace and charm. The long, elegantly proportioned room had a vaulted ceiling and walls covered with early Chinese paintings. At the far corner stood two ebony Steinways, back to back. Dr. Blitzsten was seated near one of the pianos, sipping a glass of wine. Ira was also there, along with Dr. Harvey Lewis, who soon would become a Seven Stairs "regular." After the introductions, Dr. Blitzsten asked Jennie to play for us.

I felt terribly responsible. She had scarcely touched a piano for months and I knew her extreme sensitivity as a performing artist. But she went to the piano without a word of apology and began playing Scarlatti, then an impassioned Shostakovitch prelude, and finally "The Girl with the Flaxen Hair." There was no doubt that she was accepted, and I along with her.

I went home with my book lists and the following morning was busy writing letters, opening accounts, and beginning the formation of one of the finest libraries of psychiatric books ever gathered in a single bookstore.

With Lionel Blitzsten's help, I prepared the first psychiatric book catalogue to come out of Chicago and mailed it to every psychiatrist in the United States, to every university library and institute for psychoanalysis, and to selected prospects in Canada, Brazil, Germany, even Africa. Because of Dr. Blitzsten's extraordinary editing, the catalogue featured books not readily obtained in America. I became an active importer of English titles, especially from the Hogarth Press, which had an outstanding listing of psychoanalytic books.

A few months later, I added a supplement to the original catalogue, including books on psychology, philosophy, anthropology, art and literature. I had quickly discovered that psychoanalysts were deeply interested in the impact of all areas of thought upon man's inner experience and his spiritual life. Soon ninety percent of my business was coming from my new specialty, which continued to thrive in spite of growing competition from New York involving price-cutting which the publishers appeared powerless to prevent. The local psychoanalysts were my best accounts, and many of them, including Bob

Kohrman, Harvey Lewis, Fred Robbins, Richard Renne-
ker, Aaron Hilkevitch, Jack Sparer, Joel Handler, Stan
Gamm, Ernest Rappaport and Robert Gronner, along with
Katie Dobson, the obstetrician, and Harold Laufman, the
surgeon, became torch bearers for the Seven Stairs and
lasting friends.

Even less expected than this boom in my business was
the social consequence of my deepening relationship with
Lionel Blitzsten. The last thing I would ever have con-
ceived, the last for which I would have hoped, as a consequence of my career as a personal bookseller, was an in-
duction into the Proustian world of the coterie.

The machinery of a coterie is simple; the reasons behind
its operation and its subtle influence on the lives of those
drawn into its orbit are complex almost beyond endur-
ance. Essentially, the coterie consists of a number of people who hold similiar views on unimportant things. Everyone admitted must observe a cardinal prohibition: to say
nothing fundamental about anything. All must follow
the leader, employ a common stock of expressions, adopt
the same mannerisms, profess the same prejudices, affect
the same bearing, and recognize a common bond of impenetrable superficiality.

It was all to be seen from the first, although I would
not permit my heart to acknowledge it. We were there
for the entertainment of a sick, lonely, gifted man. Sitting up in his huge bed, Lionel held forth on every subject
imaginable that related to human creativity. He talked
brilliantly, fluidly, endlessly, while his auditors listened,
sipped tea or coffee or a liqueur, bit into a cracker or sand-

wich, laughed or smiled when signaled to do so, or scowled when necessary.

The strange thing was that so many were envious and wanted desperately to belong. But the number had to be limited. Lionel did the choosing and he did the eliminating (eventually, in fact, he discarded all but one!). He used people as a machine uses oil. When a person ceased to give what he needed or showed signs of drying up, the search began for his replacement. For Lionel required constant stimulation to avoid falling into melancholy. The dinner parties and soirees to which he was addicted were at once indispensable and boring to him, tonic and yet destructive. The web of his character and his professional and social commitments was so complex that it became virtually impossible for him to find a situation of free and natural rapport or one with which he could deal in any way except capriciously. Hence his total need for the "faithful." Hence, too, if one of the "faithful" become valueless, out he went. Then began the cries and recriminations and the storm of hysteria reigned supreme in the tea cup.

One could not remain a passive spectator in this little world. If you can imagine a great hall with many rooms occupied by solitary persons somehow bound to one another by invisible, inextricable longings, with myself dashing, hopping, skipping, running from one room to another, you may have a sense of the nightmare my life was becoming — a fantasy in which some incomprehensible crisis was always arising or in which my business or personal life might be interrupted at any hour of the day or night by a call from Lionel and the despotism of his utter and absolute need.

In my heart, I knew that my dream of being the Shelley of the book business was rapidly disappearing. The act of dressing for an evening of looking at the same well-cared-for, well-groomed, vacuous people, eating the same tired hors d'oeuvres, hearing the same gossip, filled me with almost uncontrollable rage. Yet I was still caught up in the excitement of being part of this new-found pretentious world of middle-class wealth.

The first time I was really shaken was at the Christmas party. Along with others, I had helped trim the gigantic tree while Lionel sat and amused us with tales and gossip. The decorating job was truly a work of art and we were all quite pleased with ourselves when we left, the members of the inner circle lingering for a few minutes after the others were gone before offering their thanks and goodnights. We were saying our goodbyes, when Lionel turned suddenly and looked at the pillows on his huge couch.

"They haven't been fluffed up!" he said, in a voice of command.

Immediately several young analysts left their wives in the hall, dropped their coats, and rushed back to "fluff."

The whole action was so unexpected and infantile that the blood rushed to my head and for a moment I was dizzy and unable to focus. And I had let myself in for this sort of thing! Jennie and I left without saying goodnight.

"There is a time when one goes toward Lionel and another time when one goes away from him," an analyst who had once been part of the inner circle remarked. This indeed seemed to be the case, but my inner conflict remained unresolved. I was ashamed of living in a midnight of fear. At the same time I felt privileged to know this gifted and, so often, generous man, who understood the human soul as few others have. I respected and loved him and wanted to befriend him in every way that was not a violation of my own being.

As a group, I found analysts the most sensitive and intelligent to be found in the professions. But there were those I could not tolerate, no matter how much they spent at the shop; the shock artists who fed off the agony and terror of the bewildered, and the culturally illiterate who viewed anything dealing with the creative as their province. The atmosphere would begin to sizzle at the Seven Stairs the moment any of the latter started analyzing Mann, Gide, Dostoevsky, Ibsen, Kafka, Homer, anybody and everybody. I had read Freud's essay on Leonardo Da Vinci and Ernest Jones' on Hamlet with great interest and decided that the whole approach was one of intellectual gibberish, regardless of the serious intent of these great men. But the young and unread analysts were not even serious. When you cross-examined them, you found they had never read the plays or books in question: they were merely quoting an authority and taking his word for it. Of course, it is a nasty thing to expose anyone and it is sacrilegious to do it to an analyst. The change in my relations with some of the psychoanalysts became increasingly less subtle.

To offset some of the business losses attendant on this

turn of affairs, I hit on the idea of giving a series of lectures in the store after closing hours. I offered a course of five lectures on great men of literature at a subscription price of ten dollars and was surprised to find I was talking to standing room only. After a month's respite, I tried it again with similar success. Emmet Dedmon, then literary editor of the *Chicago Sun-Times* heard one of the sessions and was responsible for recommending me as a replacement for the eminent Rabbi Solomon Goldman, when he was taken sick before a lecture engagement. The success of that one lecture was such that I was booked for thirteen more. It seemed as though all was not lost.

"It's a big world," I assured myself, sitting alone in the shop before the fire. "The sun does not rise and set with a handful of analysts." It was a cool October night. Business that day had been particularly good. My debts were not pressing. I took heart.

In apparent response to this cheerful frame of mind, a smartly dressed customer entered the shop, a man of medium build with blond hair parted in the middle and a pair of the bluest eyes I had ever seen.

"I am looking for an out-of-print recording, the Variations on a Nursery Theme by Dohnanyi," he said. "Perhaps you may have it?" The accent was unmistakably British.

It was obviously my day — I did have it! "I have something else, also out-of-print, that might interest you," I said. "It's the Dohnanyi Trio, played by Heifetz, Primrose, and Feurmann."

"Oh, that," he said. "I know that one. I played it."

I hesitated, sensing some kind of ambiguity.

"I'm Primrose," he said.

We chatted while I wrapped the records. He was charmed by the shop — it had a really English flavor, he said. Before I knew it, I was telling him the whole story of the Seven Stairs.

"Until what time do you stay open?" he asked. "It's quite late."

"I'm closing right now," I said.

"If you have time, let's have a drink," he suggested. "I should like to hear more."

On a sudden inspiration, I asked first to make a phone call. While my customer browsed among the books, I spoke with Lionel and asked if he would like me to bring William Primrose over. He was ecstatic. At first note, his voice had sounded forlorn, so empty of life that I guessed him to be terribly sick. But mention of Primrose acted like a shot in the arm.

"Hurry!" he cried.

I told Mr. Primrose that my friend had a wonderful bar and a devotion to great music. But he had already heard of Dr. Blitzsten. "Isn't that the analyst?" he said. "My friends in the Budapest Quartet often used his home for rehearsal."

So off we went. Lionel was at his best — charming, informative, genuinely interested in the small talk carried on by Mr. Primrose. I was delighted really to have pleased him. When I left Primrose at his hotel that night, the world seemed good again.

Yet on the way home, I began to have hot and cold

flashes. Why had I called Lionel and offered to bring Primrose? Why?

A pleasant period followed, warmed by ripening friendships. Jennie and I attended the Primrose concert and dined with the great violist afterward. In years to come, I was to see him frequently and even present him in a memorable concert in my own shop.

While at Orchestra Hall to hear Primrose, we had also encountered Dr. Harold Laufman and his wife, Marilyn, and through some instant rapport agreed to see each other very soon. The result was an enduring friendship, as well as one of the most pleasant parties ever held at the Seven Stairs, a showing of Hal's pictures which he had painted in North Africa during the war. They were brilliant, highly individualistic works . . . "My impressions of disease," he said.

The party was a delight, particularly because there was no question of selling anything—the artist could not possibly have been persuaded to part with any of his pictures. There was nothing to do but pass out the drinks and enjoy the company, which included a lovely woman with reddish gold hair out of a Titian portrait who wanted every book and record in the shop — and who was later to deliver our first son. She was Dr. Catherine Dobson, an obstetrician, an analysand of Dr. Blitzsten, and a great and good friend.

The day after our son was born, I received a call from Lionel. "What are you going to name the baby?" he asked.

"We've decided on David," I said.

"David?" he said. "That's too plain. Why not call him Travis? I just love the name Travis."

I admitted that Travis was fine, but perhaps a bit fancy. "After all," I said, "Jennie wants to call the boy David. What's the difference?"

"A great deal of difference . . . for the boy's future," he said. "I love Travis. Suggest it to Jennie."

I had to admit to Jennie that I was afraid to take a stand. But was it too much . . . to give just a little and to keep things working for us?

"Why are you letting this man ruin our lives?" she asked.

When I couldn't answer she relented. David was named Travis David.

In the days following, I was afflicted with a recurrent rash and sometimes by mysterious feelings of terror. I had gone wrong somewhere, and a secret decision had to be made. I picked up the phone, dialed a number, and made an appointment.

I started my analysis because I was in trouble. I needed expert help and I went out and got it. Later it dawned upon me that this is really the significant thing: not that there are so many people in today's world who need help, but the miraculous urge on the part of the individual himself to get well. The fact that people on the whole don't want to be sick, don't want to be haunted by nameless difficulties, convinces me that at the very bottom of one's being is the urge to be good, to the good. This is more important than any description of the expe-

rience of analysis, which, although it may be invaluable
to the person who suffers through it, is but a process of
living . . . nothing more. After all, it was Freud who
said that life is two things: Work and Love.

As I came to tentative grips with my fears of rejection
— and the self-rejections these fears imposed — I began
more and more to act like myself, like the man who started
the Seven Stairs. If Hamlet's problem lay in his fear of
confusing reality and appearance, so, too, was mine. Only
I was not Hamlet and my task was not the avenging of a
father's murder. My task was even more basic. I had to
just keep on giving birth to myself.

It was a long time before I perceived that Lionel Blitzsten was less a cause of my problem than a factor in its
treatment. Who was this strange and often solitary genius, who died leaving such a rich legacy of interpretative
techniques to his profession, who lived like an ancient
potentate, offering to a crowd of sycophants whatever
satisfactions are to be gained from basking in reflected
glory?

My relationship with him revealed things which I was
slow in admitting to my analyst. I shall never forget the
energy I expended telling my analyst how "good" I was.
Fortunately I wasn't in the hands of a charlatan. He interrupted me — one of those rare interruptions — and
told me that we both knew how good I was, so quit wasting time and money on *that*.

Lionel was like life itself: an amalgam of selfishness,
egoism, cruelty; of goodness, gentleness, compassion. He
offered it all in almost cosmic profusion, and with cosmic

capriciousness. Once he remarked: "The world owes me nothing. When I die, I will not be sorry. I had joy, still do; I had love, still have it; I had friends, still have them. I had all and felt all and saw all and . . . believed all. I had everything and I had nothing. I had what I think life, in its total meaning, is: I had the dream, the 'chulum mensch.'"

This I believe is what he was — a "chulum mensch." It contained everything a dream could and should, good and bad. And much of it was glorious. No one who shared this part could thank him enough for the privilege of being admitted.

7

Farewell to the Seven Stairs

I HAD to break it to them gently . . . and to myself, as
well. It took a long time to compose the letter to go to all
my clients. "Sometime between June 30th and July 20th,"
the letter said, "the Seven Stairs will end its stand on Rush
Street and move to 670 North Michigan Avenue, where it
will resume life as Stuart Brent: Books and Records.

"Everything that the Seven Stairs has come to stand
for will continue. The place will be lovely and cozy and
warm — the conversations easily as crazy and possibly
more inspired. More than that — all of the wonderful
possibilities that we have been developing over the past
five years can now bear fruit."

I reviewed the history of the shop, trying to set down
some of the memorable landmarks in its growth. ". . .
and so it has gone," I wrote blithely, "always fresh and
magical, punctuated by famous and admired visitors —
Joseph Szigeti, Katharine Cornell, Elliot Paul, Ernest
Hemingway, Arthur Koestler, Frieda Fromm Reichmann,

Nelson Algren, Gore Vidal, Carol Brice, many others —
wonderful talk — parties — exhibits. You have been a
part of it with us.

"But physically, the Seven Stairs could never meet our
needs fully. It was too small. Congestion forced us to
give up those author cocktail parties for launching good
new books. It kept us from promoting lectures and exhibits. It put a definite limit to the size of our stock. And
even if we could have made more space, we couldn't have
afforded it without an increase in street trade which Rush
Street couldn't provide.

"However, for all the crowding, the worn appearance,
the careless bookkeeping, the hopeless methods of keeping
our stock of books and records in proper order — the
Seven Stairs set the tone we dreamed of.

"That tone — with all the ease and informality — will
go with it to Michigan Avenue. Probably nothing like it
has ever happened to the Avenue. It's about time it did."

My message to the faithful was heartfelt, but more than
a little disingenuous. It mentioned the economics of bookselling only in passing. And these economic factors had
at last caught up with me. I might ignore my accountant,
but when Jennie and I were invited among the well-fed
and well-cared-for, we were distinctly surrounded by the
aura of the "poor relation." I might congratulate myself
upon having accomplished, against absurd odds, so much
of what I had initially dreamed about, but I was no longer
responsible only to this dream: I had a growing family —
and I wasn't unhappy about this, either. It seemed to
me, in spite of all the evidence the modern world has to

present to the contrary, that the fullness of life (in which the feeding, clothing, and housing of a family traditionally figure) ought not, as a matter of principle, stand irrevocably opposed to personal fulfillment or spiritual realization.

There wasn't room in the Seven Stairs, it is true — for books and records, for parties, for anything else. But room is not the great necessity — it can always be made, if the spirit is willing. The plain fact of the matter was that my situation was economically self-limiting in its scope and its momentum. Only a certain number of people could be drawn into its sphere, and time and the accidents of time would take their toll. Some of the parties did not draw. Some of the clientele who dropped out or who were alienated through the vagaries of my personal relations were not replaced. I was either going to have to regress toward my beginnings or advance toward something which would suggest, at least, the possibility of greater scope.

Did this possibility exist along a well-traveled market place (the Chicago version of Fifth Avenue, although pictorially more impressive than its Manhattan counterpart), which lay only a block away from the questionable Rush Street area?

The opportunity to confront this question can e about, again, through one of the apparent accidents of life, which I identify under the rather occult heading of "attractiveness."

Without Jack Pritzker there could have been no move to Michigan Avenue. Jack and his wife, Rhoda, came into our lives at a cocktail party and became close friends.

Rhoda is English by birth and wears her charm and dignity like a delicate mystery. She has a gift for seeing and has written wonderful articles as a correspondent for British newspapers. Jack, also, has the effortless manner that stems from a quality of mind. He is as unlike me as any man can be: impassive, almost secretive, yet I have never known a more comfortable man to be with. He is a lawyer with large interests in real estate and a quiet passion for being a mover behind the success of others. He will not forsake you when the going is rough, but in his relations he holds to a fine line between friendship and duty — and holds you to this line also. I had already experienced the danger of the kind of benefactor who tends to take over your life for you but with Jack Pritzker there is never this danger. He prefers to see you make it on your own. If you are beset by circumstances which you cannot control, he is there; but if you are merely waiting for something to happen, you can expect nothing but the criticism you deserve.

This gentle, quiet man, tough yet sentimental, absorbed in his business, yet somehow viewing it as an experiment with life rather than a livelihood, devoted to concrete matters and the hard world of finance and power, yet in conversation concerned only with the breadth of life and the humanness of experience, provided a scarcely felt polarity that gave direction to my often chaotic forces.

When I heard that Jack had a financial interest in a medical office building under construction on Michigan Avenue, I asked to rent one of the street level stores. It was not a matter of seeking financial assistance — it was entirely enough to be accepted as the kind of "prestige tenant" normally sought for such a location. But when Hy Abrams, my lawyer, went to see about the lease, he reported that Jack remarked, "If you think I'm letting Stuart in this store to see him fail, you are mistaken. I have no intention of standing by and watching him and his family tenting out in Grant Park."

But even though someone might be keeping a weather eye on my survival, I had to face up to my own money problems. It is madness to go into business without a bankroll under the mattress. I thought I could see my way to making it on the Avenue, but where was the cash outlay coming from for fixtures, additional stock, everything? Not even my reformed accountant could prepare a financial statement that would qualify me for additional bank loans.

There was a way, however, and it was opened to me by a client who, as a vice president of the First National Bank of Chicago, was about the last person I thought of approaching with my difficulties. I knew about banks by now, although I had somewhat revised my opinions about the personal limitations of all bankers. In fact, it was always a source of genuine pleasure to me when this particular banker, a tall, handsome man with greying hair and a fine pair of grey eyes to match, came into the shop.

When I told him of my projected move, it was natural for him to ask how I was financing it. I told him I didn't know, but I was certainly going to have to find a way.

"May I offer a suggestion?" he said.

We sat down by the fire, and he told me first what I al-

ready knew: that normally when a businessman needs
extra money, especially for a cyclical business dependent
on certain seasons, he will go to the bank for a short-term
loan, say for ninety days. But in New York, he told me,
there is a large department store that finances its own
improvement and expansion programs. Instead of going
to the bank, the store goes to its customers. My friend
suggested that I do the same.

"Here's how it works," he said. "Write a letter to your
hundred best accounts explaining what you hope to do.
Ask them to help by sending you one hundred dollars in
advance payment against future purchases. In return,
you will offer them a twenty percent discount on all merchandise purchased under this plan. And of course they
may take as long a time as they wish in using up the
amount they have advanced."

Even as he spoke, he pulled out his pen and began
composing the letter. We worked on it for an hour, and
the next day we met at lunch to draft the final copy. I
sent the approved message to one hundred and twenty-
five people, and I received one hundred and twenty-five
replies — each with a hundred dollar check!

There remained little else to do in the way of arrangements except to break my present lease. It was not easy,
but it was a pleasure. Now that I planned to move, my
landlord's attitude was something to behold. He danced
the length of the shop on his tiny feet, his cane twirling
madly, alternating between cries of "Excellent! Your future is assured!" and "But of course you'll pay the rent
here, too!" He did not know, he said, what "the corpora-

tion" would think of any proposal for subletting the premises. Finally he doffed his black hat, waved goodbye, and skipped out of the store.

A week later I heard from him. The answer on subleasing was a qualified yes. If I could get a tenant as responsible and dignified as myself and with equally brilliant prospects for success, they would consider it.

I advertised for weeks and no such madman responded. Then one day the answer walked in the door, a huge man with the general physique of the late Sidney Greenstreet, hooded eyes, and a great beard. He looked around, blinked like an owl, and said he'd take it. It was as simple as that. I realized, with a slight sinking feeling, that I was now perfectly free to move to the Avenue.

My formidable successor to the home of the Seven Stairs turned out to indeed be a man of brilliant prospects. He opened a Thought Factory, evidenced by a sign to this effect and bulletin boards covered with slips of paper bearing thoughts. Needless to say, he was in the public relations and advertising business. I have always felt grateful to him, but I never got up courage to cross that once adored threshold and see Mr. Sperry making thoughts.

When the Columbia Record people approached me concerning the possibility of a party in connection with the release of a record by the jazz pianist, Max Miller, it struck me this might be just the thing as a rousing, and possibly rowdy, farewell to the Seven Stairs.

Somehow, when I phoned our original fellows in literature, the gaiety of my announcement did not come off. I called Bob Parrish, who had once turned an autographing party into a magic show, and was greeted by an awesome silence, followed by a lame, "We'll be there." There was similar response from others on the list, but they *did* come, all of them . . . even Samuel Putnam, who journeyed all the way from Connecticut.

We had rented a piano and managed to get it in through the back of the building by breaking through a wall. The bricks were terribly loose anyway, and it wasn't much work to put them back and replaster when it was all over. Max Miller had promised to bring along a good side man, and he did: Louis Armstrong. Armstrong was immediately comfortable in the shop. "This is a wise man," he said. He didn't know I was giving up the ghost at the Seven Stairs.

Perhaps the end of the Stairs was a symbol for more than the demise of a personal bookstore. During the period in which I had set up shop, the old *Chicago Sun* had launched the first literary Sunday supplement devoted entirely to books to be published by a newspaper outside of New York City. At least one issue of this supplement, called "Book Week," had carried more book advertising than either the *New York Times* "Book Review" or the *Herald Tribune* "Magazine of Books." The *Chicago Tribune* had followed suit with a book supplement and, together with the *Sun*, offered a platform for people like Butcher, Babcock, North, Apple, Frederick, Kogan, Wendt, Spectorsky, and others who were not only distinguished critics and authors, but who truly loved the world of books. Their efforts had certainly contributed to the climate that made the Seven Stairs possible. The diminution of this influence (today only the *Tribune* carries a full-scale book supplement) was in direct relationship to the decline of my own enterprise.

For the last party, everyone came. There were the remaining literary editors, Fanny Butcher of the *Tribune*, Emmet Dedmon of the *Sun-Times*, and Van Allen Bradley of the *Daily News* (the latter two fated to move along to editorial positions on their newspapers). There was Otto Eisenschiml and there was Olive Carrithers, for whom one of our first literary parties had been given. The psychoanalysts came: Lionel Blitzsten (who had assured everyone that I really wouldn't, couldn't, make the move), Roy Grinker, Fred Robbins, Harvey Lewis, and of course Robert Kohrman, who was still to see me through so much. There was Sidney Morris, the architect; Henry Dry, the entrepreneur; Ed Weiss, the advertising executive who discovered the subliminal world and asked which twin had the Toni; and Everett Kovler and Oscar Getz of the liquor industry. Louis played and sang and signed records and shook hands and sang some more, and Miller played and autographed while the apparent hilarity grew, the shouting, laughing, and singing. It was a very little shop, and had there been rafters you could have said it was full to them. But Ben Kartman was grim, Reuel Denny seemed bewildered, and above all, the old gang: Algren, Conroy, Parrish, Terkel, Motley, Herman Kogan . . . they were being charming and decent enough, but something was out of kilter. I had never seen them more affable, but it wasn't quite right — being affable wasn't really their line.

Terkel occasionally emerged from the throng to m.c. the

performance. Studs Terkel is a Chicago phenomenon, a talented actor and impresario of the wellsprings of culture, whether jazz or folksongs. In the early days of commercial television, when the experimenting was being done in Chicago, he created a type of entertainment perfectly adapted to the intimate nature of the medium. "Studs' Place" was the hottest show in Chicago, so far as the response of viewers went, but it soon disappeared. Apparently what Chicago offered could not be exported. The strange belief continues to persist that the tastes of America can properly be tested only on the Broadway crowd (the knowing) or the Hollywood Boulevard misfits (the paranoiac). The crowds and misfits elsewhere do not seem to constitute a suitable national index. Anyway, so far we have not been able to export Studs.

In the growing crowd and increasing turbulence and raucousness, I didn't care any longer what happened. I just stood in a corner and tried to look friendly. Rhoda and Jack Pritzker came in with a party of friends. People were crushing about Studs and Louis, urging Louis to sing and Max to play. Suddenly I was terribly tired. I wanted air. I was just getting out when the ceiling came down.

The toilet was on the second floor (it served the entire building) and, never very dependable, it had come to the end of the line. When it broke, the water came flooding down through the ceiling onto the people in the shop and taking the plaster with it. Louis was soaked. I shall always remember Rhoda Pritzker barraged by falling plaster and Dorothea Parrish losing her poise and letting out a war whoop. Studs got a piece of ceiling in his eye. Max Miller was directly beneath the broken pipe and suffered the consequences. For some moments it seemed as though the total disintegration of the aged structure was at hand.

I ran up the stairs and began applying my best flood control technique. Finally, with the aid of a pile of rags, we managed to staunch the flow. Those engaged were exhausted, but the party was made; now the laughter rang with real gaiety and the songs soared with enthusiasm. It was one hell of a wake.

The last song was "Honeysuckle Rose." The damp musicians thanked everyone for listening and said goodbye. There was a hurry of leavetaking. Soon only Ira Blitzsten, Bob Kohrman, and Ben Kartman remained.

There was nothing left but to turn off the lights and close up, yet I couldn't bring myself to rise from behind the desk. No more building inspectors, no more landlord wishing me good luck, no more broken plumbing . . . just the end of the world. All I had to do was get up, look around for the last time, turn off the lights.

Look around at what? The old bookshelves made out of third grade lumber? The dark green walls that Tweedy and Carl Dry had helped paint? The absurd little bench with its hopeful inscriptions? I didn't need to worry about the bench. I could take that with me.

There was the barrel in the corner, half full of apples . . . the battered old coffee pot sitting on the hot plate . . . and the string dangling from the ceiling from which a salami once depended. I always bought my sausage from a little old Hasidic Jew who appeared from time to time in his long black coat, black hat, and with a grey and black beard extending down his chest. We would haggle over the price and he would shower me with blessings when he left. All of this was spiced with Rabelaisian jests. Once I asked him, while studying the sausage situation, "Tell me, do you think sex is here to stay?" He thought a moment. "I don't know vy not," he said. "It's in a vunderful location!"

Somehow, I did not see a salami hanging in my new Michigan Avenue location.

But onward and upward! Don't turn back now, or Lionel's prediction will come true. All is well. The lease is signed, the fixtures are paid for, you've o.k.'d the color the walls are to be painted, no one is threatening you, and you've put down a month's advance on the rent. So please get up and turn off the lights.

It was not I, but a zombie moving mechanically toward the future, who touched the button, left the room, and softly shut the door.

8

On the Avenue

In all my life, I had never shopped on Michigan Avenue. I had no idea who was in business there or what they sold (except for a general feeling that they sold expensive merchandise and made plenty of money). It was only after I had opened the doors of Stuart Brent: Books and Records, that I discovered what a strategic location I had chosen . . . strategically in competition with two of the best-known book dealers in the city!

Only a block down the street was the Main Street Book Store, already a fixture on the Avenue for a decade. A few blocks farther south stood Kroch's, Chicago's largest bookseller and one of the greatest in America, while north of me the Michigan Avenue branch of Lyon and Healy, the great music store, still flourished. And I thought what the Avenue needed was Stuart Brent with his books and records! Maybe it was, but the outlook did not seem propitious.

Now, ten years later, Main Street and I are still selling

books and not, I think, suffering from each other's proximity. Main Street's orientation has always been toward art, and they run a distinguished gallery in connection with their business. Lyon and Healy eventually closed its branch operation, and Kroch's left the Avenue when they merged with Brentano, an equally large organization with which I have no family connection, on the Italian side or any other. These consolidations, I am sure, were simply manifestations of big business. If I were to fret about the competition, it would be that of the dime store next door, which sells books and records, too.

In addition to the street-level floor, my new shop had a fine basement room which I fitted out hopefully as a meeting place. I immediately began staging lectures and parties and put in a grand piano so we could have concerts, too. Anything to bring in people. Business grew, but as I soon found I would have to sell things besides books in order to meet the overhead, I compromised on long-standing principles and brought in greeting cards. Within six months, I was also selling "how to do it books" —how to eat, how to sleep, how to love, how to fix the leaky pipe in your basement, how to pet your cat, how to care for your dog, how to see the stars . . .

By the time I had been on the Avenue a year, it was hard for me to see how my shop differed from any other where you might find some good books and records if you looked under the pop numbers and best-sellers. Apparently some people still found a difference, however. In his book *The Literary Situation*, Malcom Cowley, the distinguished critic, wrote:

On Michigan Avenue, I passed another shop and recognized the name on the window. Although the salesroom wasn't large, it was filled with new books lining the walls or piled on tables. There were also two big racks of long-playing records, and a hidden phonograph was playing Mozart as I entered (feeling again that I was a long way from Clark and Division). The books on the shelves included almost everything published during the last two or three years that I had any curiosity about reading. In two fields the collection was especially good: psychiatry and books by Chicago authors.

I introduced myself to the proprietor, Stuart Brent, and found that he was passionately interested in books, in the solution of other people's personal problems, and in his native city. Many of his customers are young people just out of college. Sometimes they tell him about their problems and he says to them, "Read this book. You might find the answer there." He is mildly famous in the trade for his ability to sell hundreds of copies of a book that arouses his enthusiasm: for example, he had probably found more readers for Harry Stack Sullivan's *An Interpersonal Theory of Psychiatry* than any other dealer in the country, even the largest. Collections of stories are usually slow-moving items in bookstores, although they have proved to be more popular as paperbacks. One evening Brent amazed the publisher of Nelson Algren's stories, *The Neon Wilderness*, by selling a thousand copies of the hard-cover book at an autograph party.

We talked about the days when the Near North Side was full of young authors — many of whom became famous New Yorkers — and about the possibility of another Chicago renaissance, as in the years after 1915. Brent would like to do something to encourage such a movement. He complained that most of the other booksellers didn't regard themselves as integrated parts of the community and that they didn't take enough interest in the personal needs of their customers. . . . Brent's complaint against the booksellers may well have been justified, from his point of view, but a visitor wouldn't expect to find that any large professional group was marked by his combination of interest in persons, interest in the cultural welfare of the community, and abounding energy.

As a group, the booksellers I have met in many parts of the country are widely read, obliging, likable persons who regard bookselling as a profession and work hard at it, for lower incomes than they might receive from other activities. They would all like to sell more books, in quantities like those of the paperbacks in drugstores and on the news stands, but they are dealing in more expensive articles, for which the public seems to be limited.

The Literary Situation was published by Viking Press in 1954. I had met Mr. Cowley on a January evening the year before. When he came in, tall and distinguished looking, I had given him a chance to browse before asking if I could be of assistance. He smiled when I offered my help, then asked if I had a copy of *Exile's Return*. I did. He fingered the volume and asked if I made a living selling books. "Of course," I said, slightly miffed.

"But who in Chicago buys books like the ones you have on these shelves?" he asked.

"Lots and lots of people," I assured him. I still didn't know he was baiting me. We began to talk about Chicago, as I now saw it and as it had been. In a moment, he was off on Bug House Square (Chicago's miniature Hyde Park), the lamented Dill Pickle Club, the young Hemingway, Ben Hecht, Charlie MacArthur, Dreiser, Sherwood Anderson, Archibald MacLeish, Sinclair Lewis. I had to ask his name, and when he said, Malcolm Cowley, I took *Exile's Return* away from him and asked him to autograph it to me. He took the book back and wrote: "To Stuart Brent — a *real* bookstore." I felt better about being on the Avenue.

The next evening, Mr. and Mrs. Cowley came to one of our concerts in the downstairs room and heard Badura-Skoda and Irene Jonas play a duo recital.

America lacks the cafés and coffee houses that serve as literary meeting places in all European countries. I had high hopes for our basement room with its piano and hi-fi set and tables and comfortable chairs as a place for such interchange. In addition to our concerts, lectures, and art exhibits, there were Saturday afternoon gatherings of men and women from a wide range of professions and disciplines who dropped in to talk and entertain each other. We served them coffee and strudel.

Possibly the most memorable of our concerts was that played by William Primrose. He had promised long ago to do one if I ever had a shop with the facilities for it. We had them now, and quite suddenly Primrose called to announce that he would be stopping over in Chicago on his way to play with the Boston Symphony Orchestra and would be delighted to present us with a recital.

There were only a few days to prepare for the event. As soon as the word was out, we were deluged with phone calls. Our "concert hall" would seat only fifty people, so I decided to clear the floor on the street level, rent two hundred chairs for the overflow audience, and pipe the music up to them from the downstairs room. I hired a crew of experts to arrange the microphones and set up the speakers.

The show did not start with any particular aplomb, and it got worse, for me at least, as the evening progressed. Primrose came early to practice. It hadn't occurred to me that he needed to. He wanted not only to practice, but moreover a place in which he could do so undisturbed. Since the "concert hall" was swarming with electricians, not to mention the porter setting up chairs while I ran up and down the stairs alternating between a prima donna and a major domo, it looked as though another place would have to be found for Primrose to practice. I therefore took the great violist into a basement storage room that served as a catchall shared by my shop and the drugstore next door. But Primrose settled down happily in the dirty, poorly lit room amid stacks of old bills, Christmas decorations, old shelves and fixtures, empty bottles and cartons of Kleenex and went to work.

In less than ten minutes, a little grey man who filled prescriptions came bounding down the stairs screaming, "Where is Brent? Where is Brent?" He caught me in the hall and continued yelling, "If this infernal racket doesn't stop, honest to God, I'll call the police!" It was no use telling him the man making the racket was one of the world's greatest musicians. He had never heard of Primrose and couldn't have cared less. The noise coming up the vents, he claimed, was not only causing a riot in the drugstore, but he was so unnerved by the sounds that he had already ruined two prescriptions. While he was howling about his losses, I began howling with laughter. But there seemed nothing to do but get Primrose out of that room.

I moved my star into our receiving room, a messy cubby-
hole ten feet wide. He didn't seem to mind, although now,
since he couldn't walk up and down, he was confined to
sitting in a chair for his practice.

Meantime, a crowd far beyond our capacity had
swarmed into both levels of the shop. Those who came
early got seats. Others sat on the stairs leading down to
the hall. The rest stood, and some even spilled out the
door onto Michigan Avenue. I couldn't get from one end
of the place to the other without stepping on people. I
found myself begging someone's pardon all evening long.

Then the complaints began. Those seated in the hall
were gasping for air. Our cooling system simply wasn't
up to handling that many people. I rushed to the boiler
room where the gadgets for controlling the air-condition-
ing were located and tried to improve the situation. Of
course, I made it worse.

Finally I introduced Primrose to the audience and beat
a hasty retreat. Almost at once an "important" guest
tackled me with his complaints. I beat my way upstairs
(those sitting on the stairs discovered they were not able
to hear a thing) and after tripping over dozens of feet and
crushing against uncounted bodies was confronted by a
thin, long woman wearing a turban hat, who seized me
and, amid this utter confusion, began telling me I was the
most wonderful man alive. Her eyes were burning and
every time she took a breath, she rolled her tongue across
her lips. I was fascinated, but desperate. "What do you
want?" I begged, willing to do virtually anything to extricate myself. "I want you to be my agent," she said, press-

ing me to the wall. "I'm an author and I'll have nothing to do with anyone but you."

I ducked beneath her outstretched arms, trampled some people, caught my foot in the lead wire to one of the microphones, and fell heavily into the lap of one of the most attractive women I have ever seen. She fell off her chair onto the floor and I rolled on top of her. A folding chair ahead of me collapsed, and before anything could be done, a dozen lovers of music and literature lay sprawled on top of one another, while those not engaged in this chain reaction pronounced menacing "shooshes." By the time I had righted myself, several friends had come up from the concert hall to complain about the noise upstairs.

Finally the concert ended. I was later told that William Primrose gave a brilliant performance — something to be remembered and cherished for a lifetime. I would not know. All I know is that the "most attractive woman in the world" in whose lap I landed sent me a bill for eighty dollars to replace the dress which I apparently had torn beyond reconstruction. I paid the bill.

There were other fine parties, among them one that grew out of the arrival of a play called *Mrs. McThing*, a funny, whimsical, adroit production which could be the product only of a great goodness of the heart. Helen Hayes and Jules Munshin were the stars.

I loved every minute of the play, and in addition to being entranced by Miss Hayes' remarkable performance, thought Jules Munshin to be extraordinarily comical in his role. One of his telling lines was, "Let's have a meeting," no matter what the situation that provoked it. The problem might be entirely trivial, but before a decision could be made, a meeting first took place. As things do happen, the morning after the play opened in Chicago, Mr. Munshin walked into the shop along with another member of the cast. It was impossible to greet him with any other words, but, "Let's have a meeting!" We became friends instantly, and when the play neared the end of its run, we decided there should be a farewell party for the cast. Jules asked Miss Hayes if she would come, and I was properly thrilled when she agreed.

So on closing night they all came to the bookstore, along with about thirty people Jennie and I had asked to join us. The program did not have to be planned. There was singing, reciting, story-telling. Then, quite by surprise, Miss Hayes' colorful husband joined us. The fun really began, not only in heightened conversation, but when the MacArthurs' daughter sat at the piano with Chet Roble and played and sang. Roble is another Chicago "original" — an artist of the blues and a superb personality and musician who has been playing over the years at Chicago hotels and night spots and always attracts a large and appreciative following. He was part of the cast of Terkel's famous "Studs' Place'" show. He represents an almost lost art not only in his old-time jazz musicianship, but also in terms of cabaret entertainment — the performer who genuinely loves his work and his audience and who will remember ten years later the face of someone he met in a noisy night club crowd.

It was an all-night party. I talked with Miss Hayes about Ben Hecht, who had collaborated with Charles MacArthur on *The Front Page,* which opened quite a new page for the American theatre. She agreed that Ben could talk more sense, more dramatically than any author we knew. I had had an autographing party for Ben's book, *Child of a Century,* an autobiographical study of his life and development as a writer. We sold almost 800 copies of the book that night. Ben came with his wife and daughter and sat behind the desk with a cigar in his mouth, his eyes dreamy, his mind tending toward some distant land, but he was most affable, while repeating over and over: "I've never done such a thing in my whole life. And I've been writing for forty years!"

Later Hecht had taken me to the old haunts of the Chicago literary scene. We sat in a tavern he had frequented while working on the now defunct *Chicago Journal.* He showed me where Hemingway took boxing lessons. We went to the building where Ben had lived on the fourth floor and Hemingway on the floor beneath. It was a time not long past, yet far away and long ago.

We viewed the former locale of the Dill Pickle Club, the famous tavern. Ben talked to me with personal insight about Sherwood Anderson, Theodore Dreiser, Maxwell Bodenheim, Covici Friede, and others, among them, some of whose fame lay in tragic ends — death by drink, suicide, or merciless twists of fate.

Not long ago, I phoned Ben at his home in Nyack, New York. Red Quinlan, the television executive, had an idea for a series of literary shows to be called, "You Can't Go

Home Again." He had talked to me about being narrator, and I in turn had suggested Ben Hecht for the first interview.

"Ben," I said, "this is Stuart Brent. Do you remember me?"

There was a flat, "Yes," as though he didn't, really.

"I'm calling to tell you," I said, "that we have a great idea for a TV show and I want to interview you for it. It's called. . . ."

"I don't want to hear it," he said. "I don't want a living thing to do with TV. Don't tell me what you have to say. I don't want to hear it."

"Wait a minute," I said, "you haven't given me a chance."

"I don't want to give you a chance," he said. "I have no use for TV or anybody who writes for TV. It's worse than snaring little girls away from home."

"You still don't understand," I said.

"Look mister," he said, "I understand. I just don't want to hear your proposition. I want nothing to do with you or television. Is that clear?"

"Wait a minute, Ben," I said, "this is Stuart Brent from Chicago, don't you remember?"

"Oh, Stu. Where are you calling from?"

"From Chicago."

"Oh my God. Why did you let me run off like that? I thought you were some two for a nickel joker from a television agency. I'm sorry. How are you, baby?"

"Fine," I said, "but I do want to talk with you about a TV series that I hope I'm going to do."

"Sorry, baby, the answer is no. Not for any money in the world."

"Well, how are you financially?"

"Ach, you know. Same damn thing. But I don't care. I'm busy, killing myself with writing. I've got a hot book coming out soon. Be sure and get a copy. It's really hot."

"I wish you'd hear what I have to say. It's really a fine idea."

"Sorry, no. How's the bookstore?"

So we talked of books and the time I nearly blew a gasket when Ben autographed his book, *Charlie,* at another Chicago store. He had sent me a carbon copy of his manuscript on that talented and lovable bum, Charles MacArthur, and I had told him I hoped we could raise a stir with a real party when the book came out. He agreed, having been considerably impressed with the first party we held for him. Ben was in Italy writing a movie scenario when the publication date of *Charlie* was announced. Upon receiving a cablegram requesting a Chicago autographing party date, he wired, Yes, thinking it was to be at my bookstore. It wasn't . . . and for weeks after the event was held, nobody dared get near me.

"I'm still sorry about that mixup," Ben said. "Well, o.k., baby, take care of yourself. When you get to New York, give me a ring and I'll meet you for a drink at the Algonquin."

I remembered my original purpose and tried again. "For the last time, you won't listen to me about this TV thing?"

"Absolutely, irrevocably, no. Goodbye, Stu."

I was left pondering about the strange and rather terrifying creature that is Ben Hecht, a wise, witty man of the world with the disarming gentleness of a tamed jungle beast. I thought again of our sentimental revisiting of Hechtian haunts . . . the small tavern across from Bug House Square where Ben paced off the original setting: "In this corner was a stage, here were the tables, and there were the two chairs that belonged to Charlie and me. Here, in this corner, we wrote *The Front Page*."

Suddenly he put down his beer and said, "Let's take a taxi over to the campus. I want to show you where Carl Wanderer lived."

We hadn't traveled far before Ben changed the course and directed the cab driver to let us off near the Civic Opera building. We walked down a few stairs into another tavern and Ben stood, cigar in mouth, looking. There were a few men at the bar and the bartender, leaning on outspread arms and returning Ben's look inquiringly.

"Have you seen John Randolph or Michael Brown or Rudy York?" Ben said.

No one there had ever heard of them.

Ben muttered under his breath. "I guess they're all dead," he said. "I used to work with them on the *Journal American*."

We sat down and ordered a beer. "I think this must be the place," he said, "but I might have it mixed up. We had good times together. We had a real ball with this character, Wanderer. Do you know the story?

"Well, Wanderer was an ex-army officer who discovered that his wife was pregnant. He didn't want the child because he feared it would interfere with resuming his army career. He wanted to re-enlist. So he arranged for a fake holdup on Ingleside Avenue. That's where I want to take you now.

"Anyway, he got a bum off Clark Street and gave the guy a few dollars to make this holdup, assuring him it was just a trick to be played on his wife for fun. Wanderer took his wife to the movies that night, to a theatre, if my memory is correct, called the Midway. And on their way home, they have to walk almost half a block along the side of a school yard. The streets are poorly lit, and this bum sticks a gun to Wanderer and yells, 'This is a stickup!'

"The bum never had a real gun. But Wanderer did. He pretended to struggle with the guy and then shot him . . . turned the gun on his wife, too, and killed her instantly. Then he wiped off the gun and shoved it into the bum's dead hand. It looked as though the robber had been re-sisted and somehow shot in the fight. Wanderer became a hero overnight, and the newspapers played him up for all it was worth."

Ben and Carl Sandburg, who was then a reporter on the *Journal*, were eventually responsible for breaking the case. They went to interview the hero and came away with mutual misgivings which they confided to the police. It was a triumph worthy of *The Front Page*, but I think it was the irony of the world's readiness for hero worship that made pricking the Wanderer balloon such a satisfy-ing episode in the life of Ben Hecht.

In spite of all our efforts, the lectures and concerts in our downstairs room did not continue to draw indefinitely.

Sometimes we couldn't get fifty people to come out of an evening to hear good music for free (and one of the finest chamber groups in the city was providing us with a series just for the chance to play). Saturday afternoons were idle — people seemed to have become too busy to spend time in simple conversation.

Book sales dropped, too. Price cutting hurt the psychiatric mail order business, although we held out for several years. Finally we discontinued the catalogue, in spite of its definitive value as a listing of significant books in this field.

Again, something new had to be done and done quickly. I decided to go after business and industrial accounts and to persuade them to give books instead of whiskey for Christmas presents. My successes included selling a bank 250 copies of the Columbia Encyclopedia, with the name of each recipient stamped in gold on the cover. I'm not sure this did much for the human spirit, but it helped pay the rent.

One afternoon Ben Kartman came in with a friend who had some ideas about Brent and television. They arranged an audition, I was accepted, and for almost a year I had a fifteen minute afternoon show, sandwiched between a program on nursing and one on cooking. Financially it was a disaster. I was paid scale, which at that time was $120 per week, and after I paid my union dues and my agent's fees, most of the cost of the extra help I had to hire to cover the shop during my absences came right out of my own pocket. But I did learn this: be very careful what you sign, re-read the small print, and be sure to see your lawyer — lessons that would be helpful when television again beckoned in ways to be fully described in another chapter.

Every morning as I turned the key in the lock and entered the shop, my heart sank. Each day brought trouble, process servers, trips to the lawyer. This was what came from entering a retail business without a financial "cushion"—and especially a business that demanded a large stock: for every book I sold, I had to buy three . . . three books it might take months to sell. Sometimes I could visualize the credit managers sitting down for a meeting—their agenda: Let's Get Brent. There was nothing to do but fight it out, worry it out, dream it out.

I have said disparaging things about the publishing industry and shall say more. But it was publishers and their representatives who, in large measure, saw me through. There was Robert Fitzhenry from Harper, now some kind of an executive, then one of the top salesmen in the business. He reminded one of Hemingway's description of Algren: watch out for him or he will kill you with a punch. At one time you'd have thought from the titles on the shelves that I was a branch store for Harper. There was Joe Reiner from Crown Publishers, one of the first to sell me books out of New York. He too has graduated into the executive category. He taught me many things about the book business, and it was he who arranged for me to buy old book fixtures from the late Dorothy Gottlieb, the vivid, marvelous proprietress of the Ambassador Bookstore.

Bennett Cerf, master showman of the industry, gave me a measure of prestige when I needed it by making me an editor, along with Jessie Stein, of the Psychiatric Division of Random House. I was able to help their list with a number of important works by Chicago analysts.

Over the years people like Ken McCormick, Michael Bessie, Pat Knopf, Jr., Ed Hodge, Richard Grossman, Gene Healy, Peter Fields, Bob Gurney, Max Meyerson, Bella Mell, Bill Fallon, and Hardwick Moseley became more than business acquaintances and left their imprint on my life as well as upon my adventures in the book world. But more about that world later.

As business improved and as the light gradually became visible through the turbid waters in which I seemed immersed, my energies became increasingly focused upon the simple matter of keeping going, the business of each day's problems, each month's decisions, each year's gains. Work and living have a way of closing in around one's being so completely that when fate strikes through this envelopment, it comes as a stunning surprise. Fate does not care for what has been the object of one's personal concern, and it seldom sends a letter or telegram to announce its arrival.

It had been just another day. Jennie had complained of a headache and some difficulty in focusing. In the afternoon we saw a doctor and in the evening an eye specialist. Evidently it was not glaucoma. Nonetheless we administered some eye drops and some pills. I fell asleep in the living room in my chair that night and was awakened early in the morning by three small children, vaguely perturbed, dragging their blankets behind them. Jennie was dead.

Death is not saying goodbye. One can no more say goodbye to death than to a statue or a wall. There is nothing to say goodbye to. It is too natural and final to be dealt with in any of the artificial, temporizing ways with which we pretend to conduct relations with reality.

My first impulse was to run — sell the store for whatever I could get, pack up my things, and leave. Take off perhaps for the little fishing village of Bark Point on the Northern tip of Wisconsin where we had a summer place and there retire in solitude and raise the children as best I could.

It was Bob Kohrman who got me to quit trying to react to death and to just go ahead and mourn. Death has no face, is no audience, has nothing to do with reaction. It is the life of the individual that demands everything, cries out to be lived, and if mourning is a part of this, go ahead. So I stayed where I was and worked and mourned, until one day the pain of loss stopped altogether.

Michael Seller had come over to the apartment one night and talked to me. "For one thing," he begged, "don't let irritations and problems pile up. Resolve them from day to day. And another thing . . . no matter what the cost, come home every night for supper. Never let a day or night go by without seeing your children and talking with them."

I followed Mike's advice to the letter. Every night I was home for dinner at six o'clock, even though I might have to leave later and return to the store. My routine was established. I ate, slept, and worked, and after store hours I gave myself to the problems that beset all parents of small children: changing diapers and being concerned over unexpected rashes and fevers in the night. I remembered Tolstoy's answer to the question: When is a man free? A man is free when he recognizes his burden, like the ox that recognizes its yoke.

I learned that I was not alone. It was not only old friends like Claire Sampson bringing over a turkey for our dinner, or Lollie Wexler, early one wintry morning unbuttoning the hood about her blonde hair and, flushed with the cold and her own tremendous effort, saying ever so softly, "Can I help?" It was also people I scarcely knew, such as the strange man whose name I invariably forgot, but who dressed so elegantly, a stickpin in his tie, his moustache beautifully trimmed, a small flower in his lapel, and who called everybody, "Kid." He came in now on a wet November night and bought some detective stories. To my astonishment, when I handed him the books, he began to weep. The tears were irresistible, so I looked at him and wept also. "You're a sweet kid," he said, strangling, and turned and left the shop.

There was Marvin Glass, a genius at toy design, devoted like Mann's Herr Settembrini to the total encompassment of human knowledge. I almost had to hire a girl to take care of his special orders alone, dispatching telegrams, night letters, even cablegrams for books he wanted yesterday. He spoke in confidential whispers, but his expression was always so precise that you invariably found yourself watching carefully over every word you uttered in response.

There was Bert Liss, who wore the most beautiful coats

I had ever seen and a fantastic series of elegant hats: a Tyrolean hat, a checkered cap, a Cossack fur hat, a dashing black homburg. Whenever he went crazy over a book, at least twenty of his friends would order a copy. But more than that, he was a gentleman, firm in his belief in the goodness of man.

Sidney Morris, the architect who helped design the interior of the shop (and never sent a bill) was there, not only to buy, but more important, whenever I needed someone to confide in. There was Oscar Getz — Oscar, in vaguely Prince Albert dress, forgetting a life of business and civic responsibility the moment he entered the world of letters. Upon encounter with ideas, his eyes lit up and his body began to quiver. There was no doubt about his ability to entrance his listeners. Once, while driving him home after an evening spent at a small cafe listening to gypsy music, I became so absorbed in what he was saying that I was presented with tickets for two traffic violations, one for failing to stop at a red light and another for going in the wrong direction down a one-way street.

Another scholarly business man, Philip Pinsof, came in with his brothers, Oscar and Eddie, and together they made it clear that I was being cared for. In later years I was to enjoy Sabbath dinners at the Pinsofs' — where Phil's wife was a most gracious hostess who would seat her husband on a red pillow, as if to say, "For five days you have received the slings and arrows of the marketplace, but on Friday night you are as a king in your own home."

George Lurie came not only to buy books but to regale me with stories, such as the episode in which he attended the board of governors meeting of a major university and was invited to sign a book in which each guest had inscribed not only his name but his alma mater. George wrote his name in the book and cryptically added H & M. The gentleman sitting next to him asked, "Harvard and what? Massachusetts Institute of Technology?" "No," said George, "Halsted and Maxwell" — the address of Chicago's famous and still extant open air market.

Everett Kovler, president of the . Jim Beam whiskey company, made it clear to me that I could call him and say, "Everett, I need a sale." There were times when I did, and he always replied, "Fine, send it." Another official of the same firm, George Gabor, was also my benefactor. Through a strange twist of fate, he was able to cancel a debt that plagued me, muttering under his breath as he bought a book, "About that . . . it's all been washed out."

While the kindness of my customers served to cheer my heart no little, my peace of mind was greatly augmented by the personal friendship and professional concern of Dr. Arthur Shafton, the kind of pediatrician who would come to the house at a moment's notice to treat bleeding or feverish children and soothe their hysterical father, the kind of physician who views medicine as an art. Sometimes when he dropped into the shop, he would take me in hand too, suggesting, "Perhaps you ought to go home now, you look tired."

For a brief time, I also thought I had found a gem of an

office girl. She was certainly unique and physically strik-
ing: a high breasted young creature at least six feet tall
who responded to instructions by taking a deep breath,
blinking her grey-blue eyes, and intoning, "Will do!"
Then she would wheel on her spike heels, pick up her
knees with an elevation that threatened to strike her chin,
and walk away, a marvel of strange symmetry. She was
the most obedient employee I ever had and the tidiest.
My desk was always clean as a whistle. But when the
time came for the month's billings, I could find no accounts. I rushed to Miss "Will do" in consternation. She
fluttered her lashes and said, "I threw them away." That
was how she kept my desk so clean!

As Christmas approached, the consideration and gen-
erosity of my friends and customers became positively or-
giastic. Ruth Weiss called and said, "I'm telling everyone
I know to send books and records for Christmas," and apparently they did so. I have never seen so many art books
sold at one time as on the day Dr. Freund and his wife,
Geraldine, came in. Dr. Freund kept saying, "Lovely, I
must have it," to everything I showed him, until I became
thoroughly embarrassed, and still he persisted in buying
more. Sidney Morris sent books to all his architect friends,
and the purchases of Morry Rosenfeld were so prodigious
that Mae Goodman, my floor manager, was left speech-
less. The gentle Ira Rubel spent hours making copious selections, saying quizzically of each purchase, "Do you
really think this is the most suitable?" A. N. Pritzker,
Jack's brother, made one of his rare appearances, and
bought records — a little classical, a little operatic, a little

ballet, a little jazz, a little popular, until he had a stack three feet high which he insisted upon paying for on the spot, although we were really too busy to figure up the amount.

It went like this day after day, until my embarrassment at so much kindness, and my inability to know what to say or do about it, became almost too much. Late at night, I would lie awake thinking about all these people rallying about me. And then my embarrassment turned to humble acceptance of so much caring, so much human warmth.

9

Bark Point

WHENEVER I travel, one thing is certain: that I will get lost. Perhaps if I could remember which is my right hand and which is my left, or tell north from south, I should be able to follow directions more successfully. But it probably wouldn't help. I have an unfailing knack for choosing the wrong turn and a constitutional incapacity for noticing important signs.

It was therefore not surprising that, on a summer twelve years ago, while making my way toward Canada, I turned up Bark Bay Road thinking I had found a shortcut and very nearly drove off a cliff overhanging Lake Superior. Berating myself as usual, I looked around and observed a man working in a field not far from the road. He wore a battered felt hat, a shirt open at the neck, heavy black trousers supported by suspenders, and strong boots. His eyes were sky blue and his weathered skin, brown as a nut, was creased in a myriad of wrinkles on the neck and about the eyes. When I approached and asked him how to get to Canada, he replied in an accent that I could not place. His speech was rapid and somewhat harsh in tonality, but his manner was cheerful and friendly, so I paused to chat with him. He said he was preparing his strawberry field for next year.

"This is beautiful country," I said.

"Ya, it is that," he said.

"I wish I owned some of it," I said. "I think I could live here for the rest of my life."

"Well, this land belongs to me. I might sell you an acre, if you like."

As we walked across the field toward the bay, he said, "Are you a son of Abraham?"

I had never been called anything that sounded quite so beautiful. "Yes, I am a son of Abraham," I said proudly.

"My name is Waino," he said. "I am a fisherman. But I own this land."

Trees, grass, and water . . . there was nothing else to be seen, except a small house covered with flowers and vines a quarter mile across a clover field. "Who lives there?" I said.

"My brother-in-law, Mike Mattson. He might sell you his house," Waino said.

I met the Mattsons. Mike looked kindly. His eyes were grey rather than blue, but his skin was as deeply brown as Waino's, with as many crinkles about the eyes. Waino's sister, Fanny, wore a kerchief about her head, tied with a small knot beneath her chin. She spoke little English and our business transaction was often interupted while Mike translated for her in Finnish.

I bought the house and an acre of ground. The house had only two small rooms, no running water, no toilet. This didn't matter. Like the room that originally housed the Seven Stairs, *I wanted it.* I had the identical feeling: no matter what the cost, or how great the effort and sacrifice that might be entailed, this place must be mine. My soul stirred with nameless wonder. I felt lifted into the air, my life charged with new purpose and meaning. I put down one hundred dollars as earnest money, arranged a contract for monthly payments, and became a part of Bark Point.

Bark Point is located at the northernmost corner of Wisconsin. At this writing, exactly five people live there the year around. In summer, the Brents arrive, and our neighbors, Clay Dana, Victor Markkulla, Robert McElroy, Waino Wilson and the Mike Mattsons, swelling the total population to as many as fifteen adults and children. The nearest town, Herbster, is six miles away. Farther south is the town of Cornucopia, and to the north, Port Wing. Thirty-five miles off the coast of Lake Superior stand the Apostle Islands, and beyond, Canada. It is about as far from Michigan Avenue as you can get.

This new habitat which I grasped so impulsively provided a kind of spiritual nourishment which the city did not offer. And later when I married Hope, she responded as eagerly as I had to the benign sustenance of this isolated sanctuary.

It is not only the natural beauty and quiet remoteness of the locale, but also the strength that we find in association with our neighbors, whose simplicity stems not from

lack of sophistication, but from the directness of their relations with the forces of life and nature.

There is John Roman, who lives in Cornucopia, the tall,
thin, master fisherman of the Northern world. He is gentle, shy, and rather sensitive, with the courage of one who
has been in constant battle against nature, and the wisdom given only to those who have endured the privations
and troubles and disappointments of life completely on
their own. Now well into his seventies, he fishes a little
for pleasure, cuts pulp to make a few dollars, and spends
much of his time listening to foreign news reports on his
short wave radio.

When he stops by for his glass of tea, he never comes
empty handed. There is always something wrapped in a
newspaper to be presented to you in an off-hand manner,
as though to say, Please don't make a fuss about this . . .
just put them in your freezer until you are ready to eat
them. The package, of course, contains trout. When no
one else can catch trout, John Roman can. He knows
every lake and river and brook and he uses nothing but
worms to bait his handmade fishing rod and gear. So
far as John is concerned, there isn't a fish swimming that
won't take a worm. He has caught trout that weighed
fifty pounds, and once he tangled with a sturgeon that
wanted to carry him to the bottom of the lake — and could
have.

The sturgeon encounter occurred about eight miles
from our house on a lake called Siskwit that is filled with
walleyes, bass, some smaller pan fish, and sturgeon. One
morning while fishing alone in his boat, John thought his

hook had caught on a sunken log or rock. He edged the boat forward slowly, dragging the hook, but nothing gave. He moved the boat backward. Still no give. Finally John had a feeling that he could reel up. He could, but only very slowly. Then all at once, the sturgeon came straight up from the water, looked at John, then dove straight down, and the boat began to tip and go down, too. John promptly cut the line. He is a regular Old Man of the Sea, but he found no point, he said, in trying to land a fish weighing perhaps two hundred pounds. The thing to do when you are outmatched is cut the line.

John has met the problems of his own life, but the reports of the world concern him. The danger of Fascists appearing in the guise of saviors of democracy worries him. He senses that men are losing their grip on values and are in for a hard time. But what he cannot understand are the reasons for moral apathy. If an "ignorant" man in the North woods can see trouble at hand, is it possible, he wonders, that others do not?

Bill Roman is one of John's sons and the husband of Waino's only daughter, Lila. Bill used to run the filling station in Cornucopia. Now he builds houses. But his real genius lies in his understanding of boats and the water. He would advise me: "Look at the barometer every morning before you go out and believe it. If you're caught in a sudden squall, slow the motor and head for the nearest shore. Don't go against the wind. Stay in the wake of the waves. Don't buck the rollers and don't be proud. Keep calm and get into shore no matter where it might be." Bill is known for fabulous skill in getting out of tight squeezes, and his advice is good enough for me.

He is also the only man I have known who could properly be described as innocent. His philosophy of life is built upon an utter incapacity to be moved by greed or ambition. "Just live," he keeps saying. "Just live. Don't fight it. Don't compete. If you don't like what you are doing, change. Don't be afraid to change. Live in harmony with what you are and what you've got. Don't fight your abilities. Use them. I like living and I like to see others live."

Bill tries to get on, so far as possible, without money — and with Bill that is pretty far. "I try to never think about money," he says. "When you start thinking about money, you get upset. It hurts you. That's why I like Bark Point, where we can live simply. I got my health, my wife, my boy. I got my life. I don't believe in success or failure. I believe in life. I build for others and do the best I know how. I listen to music on the radio. I go fishing. Every day I learn something. Books are hard to come by here, but I have re-read everything we've got. And I love the winters here better than the summers. In the winter we can see more of our friends and sit and talk.

"But money is evil. Money and ambition. Money always worries me. I'm glad I'm without it. I have enough without it. What I want, I can have. But the secret is to know what to want."

Over the years, we built additions to the house until there were enough bedrooms for all of us, a sitting room with a magnificent fireplace, and even a Finnish bath-house, called a sauna. We enjoy taking steam baths and have discovered the children do, too.

Raspberries and blueberries grow by the carload in our field, there are apples on the trees and Sebago Salmon in our lake. This particular salmon is a landlocked fish, generally weighing between five and six pounds and very handsome. His skin is covered with silver crosses, he has a short, hooked mouth, and his flesh is orange. He is caught by trolling.

A few miles from our house are rivers and streams sel-dom discovered by tourists. Hence we can catch rain-bows weighing four and five pounds and browns often weighing more. We have lakes where we can catch Northerns weighing twenty, thirty, forty pounds, and walleyes by droves. We can take you to a lake where you can catch a fish in one minute — not very big, but a variety of pan fish seldom seen or caught anywhere else. We can take you to a trout stream where you can fish today, come back next week, and find your footprints still in the sand, utterly unmolested.

It is a land of beauty and plenty, but nature is not soft. Sometimes a Northeaster will blow for five days at a time. Then you can stand at the window and watch the lake turn into something of monumental ferocity, driving all human endeavor from the scene. Trees are uprooted, win-dows are smashed, telephone wires and power lines are downed. Lightning slashes, the rumbling of thunder is cataclysmic, and the rain comes. Often Waino would call and warn of an impending storm and the necessity of securing the boat with heavy rope. But sometimes it was

too late, and we would have to go out in the teeth of the
early storm to do battle, rushing down the beach in our
heavy boots, heads covered with oilskins, beating against
the rising wind whose force took the breath out of you.
But the roaring surf, the lashing rain, the wind tearing at
every step, are tonic to the blood!

One night while standing at the window watching the
hard rain falling on the Bay, I was suddenly alerted to action by the sight of water rushing over the embankment
which we had just planted with juniper. The torrent of
water washing away the earth was obviously going to
carry the young juniper plants along with it. There was
only one thing to do and it had to be done at once: cut a
canal in the path of the onrushing water to channel the
flood in a different direction.

Hope was napping. I awoke her, and armed with shov-
els, we pitted ourselves against the storm. At once we
were up to our ankles in mud. Hope's boots stuck and,
being heavy with child, she was unable to extricate herself. My tugging only made matters worse and, with
shouts of anguish, we both toppled over into the mud.
But no damage was done and, muddy from head to foot,
wallowing in a slough of muck, laughing and gesturing
and shouting commands at each other, we got on with
cutting the canal. It was mean work, but there was something exhilarating about it all and, when the challenge
was successfully met and we were in by the fire, quietly
drinking hot chocolate, a kind of grave satisfaction in
knowing that this was in the nature of things up here and
that we had responded to it as we should.

Bark Point is a good place for growing children as well

as for tired adults. It is good for children to spend some time in a place where a phrase such as "know the score" is never heard, where nobody is out to win first prize, where nobody is being urged continually to do something and do it better, and where the environment is not a constant assault upon quietness of the spirit. Children as well as adults need to spend periods in a non-communicative and non-competitive atmosphere. I am opposed to all those camps and summer resorts set up to keep the child engaged in a continuous round of play activities, give the body all it wants, and pretend that an inner life doesn't exist.

At Bark Point, our children can learn something first hand about the earth, the sky, the water. They plant and watch things grow, build and watch things form. There is no schedule and no routine, but every day is a busy day, filled with natural activities that spring from inward urgings, and the play they engage in is something indigenous to themselves.

Before the lamprey eels decimated the Lake trout, most of the men in the Bark Point area fished for a living. Years ago, I was told, Bark Point boasted a school, a town hall, a general store, even a post office. But now commercial fishing is almost at an end — the fine Lake Superior trout and whitefish are too scarce. So the bustle of the once thriving fishing village is gone, along with the anxious watch by those on shore when a storm comes up. No need for concern now. Let it blow. No one is fishing.

Almost no one. But the few remain — marvelous, jolly

fellows, rich with earthy humor, strong, dependable, completely individualistic. Every other morning they take their boats far out in the lake and lift the Pon Nets. It is dangerous work, and thrilling, too, when from two to three hundred pounds of whitefish and trout are caught in one haul.

Nearly everyone is related and most of the children have the same blue eyes and straw hair. But the children grow up and discover there is nothing for them to do. Fishing is finished, and about all that is left is to cut pulp in the woods or become a handy man around one of the towns. Farming is difficult. The season is so very short and considerable capital is required to go into farming on any large scale. Nobody has this kind of money.

Then, too, the old folk were beginning to hear for the first time a new theme: the work is too hard. For a time, this filled them with consternation. But they recognized the sign of the times and even came to accept it. The young people no longer were interested in working fifteen and sixteen hours a day as their fathers had. They left their homes and went to Superior or Duluth or St. Paul or much farther. The few that remained stayed out of sheer bullheadedness or innate wisdom. It was an almost deserted place when I found it, and it has remained so all these years.

Those who stayed became my friends and their world is one I am proud and grateful to have entered. I have played cribbage and horseshoes with them, gone with them on picnics and outings, fished all day and sometimes late at night. We have eaten, played, and worked together, but most important to me has been listening to them talk. Their conversation is direct, searching, and terribly honest. Many of their questions bring pain, they strike so keenly upon the wrongs in our world. I am used to answering complicated questions — theirs possess the simplicity that comes directly from the heart. Those are the unanswerable questions.

I would often sit with them in dead silence around the fire, five or six men dressed in rough clothing, their powerful frames relaxed over a bottle of beer or a glass of tea, each lost in his own thoughts. But this silence wasn't heavy — it was an alive silence. And when someone spoke, it was not to engage in nonsense. Never have I heard commonness or cheapness enter into their conversation. When they talked, what they said had meaning. It told something. A cow was sick. An axle from a car or a truck or a tractor broke. The nets split in two. Soon the herring season will be upon us. What partnerships will be entered into this year? The weather is too dry or too rainy. Someone is building a shed or a house. Someone cut his thigh and needed thirty stitches. Someone needs help in bringing in his hay.

In this world that is entirely elemental, each man wrestles with the direct necessities of living. This is not conducive to small talk, to worrying about losing a pound or gaining a pound or figuring out where to spend one's free time. When there *is* time for relaxation, the talk usually turns to old times, fables of the world as it "used to be" — the giant fish once caught: rainbows weighing fifty pounds, browns weighing seventy, steelheads by the

droves. And behind all of this lies the constant awareness that Lake Superior is an ocean, never to be trifled
with, never taken for granted.

The women are strongly built and beautiful, with low,
almost singsong voices. Their "yes" is a "yah" so sweetly
inflected that you want immediately to imitate it, and
can't. Their simple homes are handsomely furnished
through their own labors. When I dropped in, unexpected, I was certain to receive a quiet, sincere greeting
that put me at ease and assured me I was no intruder.
There would be a glass of tea or coffee and a thick slice
of home-made bread spread with butter and a variety of
jams. Nearly everything in the household was made by
hand, all the clothing, even the shoes. And just about
everything outside the household, too, including the fine
boats.

Even today it is possible to live like a king at Bark
Point on fifteen hundred dollars a year — under one
condition: one must learn to endure loneliness and one
must be capable of doing things for himself.

The people around Bark Point have radios and television sets, automobiles and tractors and other machines.
But the people come first, the machines second. Bark
Point people do not waste time questioning existence.
They laugh and eat and sleep without resorting to pills.
They have learned to renounce and to accept, but there is
no room in their lives for resignation and pessimism. However, they do suspect that the world outside is mostly populated by madmen, or, as one of my neighbors said to
me, "What do you call dogs that foam at the mouth?"

When I go to Bark Point, it occurs to me that what the world needs is more private clubs, more private estates and exclusive residential areas, more private centers of entertainment, anything that will isolate the crass from the mainstream of life and let them feed upon themselves. Anything that will keep them away from the people of Bark Point.

The master builder of Bark Point is a seventy-seven year old man named Matt Leppalla. When one asks Matt a question, his invariable reply is, "I'll look of it." "Look of it" means that he will measure the problem, work it in his mind, and provide the answer. He lives in a house built entirely by his own hands. If he needs a tool for a job and no such tool exists, he invents it. His energy and capacity for sustained work is amazing for a man of any age. He has built almost everything we possess at Bark Point.

A few summers ago, we decided to build a dock to protect our beach and secure our boat against the fierce Northeaster. So Matt and I took the boat and set out to look for logs washed up on the shores of Bark Bay. There was no hesitation on Matt's part as we hurried from log to log. "Good," he would say, "this is cedar. No good, this is poplar. This is good. This is Norway pine. No good, this is rotten in the middle." And so from log to log, Matt in the lead with the canthook on his back and with me following behind, trying as hard as I could to keep up.

When the selection had been made, Matt offered to teach me how to tie the logs so we could tow them over the lake to our shore. It looked easy, but it required an

almost occult knowledge of weights and forces to deter-
mine exactly the right place to tie the rope so the log
would not slip and jam the motor or slam against the side
of the boat. Everything there is to be known about leverage Matt knows, including the most subtle use of ropes
and pulleys for least expense to the human back.

The building of the crib for our dock was one of the
wonders of the world, executed with the quickness and
sureness of a man who knows and loves what he is doing.
Or if any difficulty arose with material too stubborn to
bend to his thinking, I could virtually see him recast his
thought to fit the situation.

Matt is slight of build and the eyes behind his spectacles
are sparkling blue. When he first got the glasses, they
were not fitted to his satisfaction, so he improved them by
grinding the lenses himself. He reminds me in many ways
of my own father, who had a bit of Matt's genius and ver-
satility. When I see Matt work, I seem to see my father
again . . . building, planning, dreaming, trying to make
something out of nothing.

Ervin owns the general store in Herbster. Every week
he drives his truck to Duluth for supplies, carrying with
him a frayed, pocket-sized notebook in which he has written down everything people have asked for. Once I had
a chance to look through this notebook which Ervin treas-
ures with his life. Only Ervin could possibly know what
was written in it.

Ervin's capacity for eating is marvelous to behold.

While the children stare at him in petrified wonder, he will put together a sandwich of cheese, sausage, fish, butter, meat balls, even strips of raw meat. His capacity for work is equally limitless. He is a powerful man and can wrestle with bags of cement all day long. But he cannot catch fish! At least that is his story and his claim to fame in the area: never to have caught a fish that amounted to anything. I don't believe a word of it.

Ervin fights many of the same business battles I have fought with no capital and extended credit. He worries about it, but the odds are a challenge to him. You cannot long endure at Bark Point unless you are capable of meeting challenges.

In addition to his appalling eating habits, Ervin chews tobacco and is a horrifying master of the art. He showed our boys the full range of techniques employed for spitting out of a fast-moving truck, and they thought it was wonderful. But he has also taught them all about the bears and deer and foxes and wolves and other wild life that abound in our forest. He helped me with the plans for our house, with the boat, with the art of reading a compass, and with the geography of the myriad lakes and streams hidden throughout the area. Ervin knows everything and says very little. He is easy to be with, and a solid friendship based upon mutual respect has grown between us.

When spring begins to come, something that has been kept buried in our winter hearts can no longer be suppressed. The children start saying, "We'll be leaving for Bark Point soon, won't we?" One spring day when the

children were on vacation from school, I packed the boys
into the car and we set out for an early visit to our spiritual
home. The day of our arrival was clear and beautiful.
The ice had gone out of the Bay and clumps of snow remained only here and there. New grass was coming up
from the steaming earth. There were pink-flecked clouds
in the sky and a glorious smell everywhere that filled us
both with peace and exhilaration.

But early the next morning it began to snow, coming
down so thick and fast it was a sight to behold. My exclusively summer experience of the North Country
warned me of nothing. We delighted in the snowy wonderland seen from the snugness of the house, and bundled
up in heavy clothes and boots to go out and revel in it.

It snowed all through the night. On the following morning, it seemed to be coming on stronger than ever.
I phoned Ervin — fortunately the telephone lines were
still working. He thought the snow might stop by evening.

"How are your supplies?" he said.

"Still o.k.," I said.

"What about fuel?"

"Waino gave me a supply of wood and brickettes for
the stove yesterday."

"Have you got enough?"

"Yes — so far."

"Good. As soon as it stops, I'll be up with the truck."

But the snow did not stop. The following day it lay ten
feet high and was still coming.

Ervin called again. "The roads are closed," he said. "I
can't get to you. Can you hold out?"

"Yes," I said, "but I'm starting to cut up the furniture for the stove and I'm worried about the children."

"I'll come up the minute I can get there," he said, "but I can't do nothing about it yet."

It snowed for three days and three nights without a letup. I tried to keep awake, dozing in a chair, never daring to let the fire go out. We had long since run out of fuel oil, but luckily we had the wood-burning cook stove. I broke up two tables, all the chairs, and was ruefully contemplating the wooden dresser. The phone had gone dead and we were completely isolated.

It was night, the snow was up to the windows and it was still coming on — a dark world shot with white flecks dancing and swirling. The whole thing seemed completely impossible. But it was happening and there was nothing to do but wait it out.

We had no milk, but there was water and a small supply of tea and coffee. There was flour, too, and we made bread . . . bread without yeast or salt. It tasted terrible, but we ate it and laughed about it. I read or played cribbage with the boys. They played with their fishing reels, oiled them, took them apart, put them back together, took them apart again. We waited.

The morning the snow stopped we were greeted by bright sunlight hot on the window panes. Everyone jumped up and down and yelled, "Yay!"

But how to get out of the house? We were snowed in completely.

About noon, Ervin called. The lines were fixed and Bill Luoma was working like crazy with his tractor opening the Bark Bay Road. Everyone had been alerted to our plight and help would be on the way.

Several more hours passed. We were without food or fuel, and I still hated the idea of chopping up that dresser. Then all at once our savior was in sight: Ervin in his truck, way down the main road and still unable to get anywhere near our driveway.

There was no restraining the children in their excitement. The yelling and shouting was enough to waken the dead. I found myself laughing and yelling, too, and waving madly to Ervin. We were all behaving as though we were going to a picnic instead of getting out of a frightful jam.

Finally Bill came lumbering up the road with his snow plow and in fifteen minutes cut a huge pathway to the house. We came out and danced around Ervin's truck as it backed slowly into the driveway.

"Where's your car?" Ervin asked.

We had to look around — it was completely buried. I had even forgotten I had it. Working together, we cleared the snow away. I tried starting the motor, but nothing happened. Ervin attached a chain to the car and pulled it up the road. This time the motor turned over, but so suddenly (and my reflexes were so slow) that, before I knew it, the car had swerved off the wet road into a ditch. I was fit to be tied.

Getting the car onto the road from the muddy embankment took an hour. Finally it was done and all was well. We retired to the house and made a feast of the supplies Ervin had brought, eating as though we were never likely to see food again, building Ervin-style sandwiches and consuming them with Ervin gusto. Occasionally Ervin would cast around and say something droll about the absence of chairs and having to sit on the edge of a dresser. Everything seemed hilariously funny. It was the best party I ever had.

When June arrives, we organize our caravan and steal away in the early hours of the morning: six children, the maid, two cats, three birds, two Golden Retrievers, Hope and I and all the luggage, packed into a station wagon. Gypsies have to get out of town while the city sleeps.

At first our spirits are high. The babies, Amy and Lisa, play or sit quietly. Then restlessness sets in. David and Jonathan become fidgety. David playfully slaps Jonathan, and the battle begins. I lose my temper and bawl at both of them. Then Lisa gets tired and tries to sleep on Hope and Amy and me in the front seat. Now Susan wants some water, and David calls out from the back of the wagon, "I'm sick." Amy now wants to sleep, too, so in the front seat we have: me at the wheel, Lisa, Amy, Hope, and Big Joe in Hope's arms. In the center of the car are Susan, the maid, and the two dogs; in the back, David and Jonathan, the birds and the cats, and everything that we couldn't tie on top in the luggage carrier.

But we are off! And amid confusion and frayed nerves — and much laughter, also — we share a secret joy, a gypsy joy, and the knowledge that our spiritual refuge lies ahead and so many useless cares and dehumanizing pressures drop farther and farther behind us.

Where it all began.

Stuart Brent.

Fanny Butcher, literary critic; Bennett Cerf, publisher; Jenny
Brent; Stuart Brent.

Ben Hecht and Stuart Brent.

Stuart Brent lecturing at The Seven Stairs.

"For Stuart and Jenny, the cats with the golden hearts, from Uncle Nels with all fond wishes."

Nelson's birthday party with (*left to right*) Studs Terkel, Robert Parrish, Stephen Spender, Stuart Brent, Jack Conroy, Nelson Algren.

ROBERT McCULLOUGH

Louis "Satchmo" Armstrong and Stuart Brent.

The Seven Stairs was mentioned in *Life* when *The Old Man and the Sea* was published.

Ben Kartman,
Stuart Brent,
Studs Terkel.

Stuart Brent with
Toast, hero of
three children's
books.

Richard Stern and Saul Bellow.

Prima ballerina Natalia Makarova and Stuart Brent.

At home in the country.

Bill Roman, who has made an art of living life simply, worries about the inroads of those who seem determined to despoil what remains of this crude but civilized outpost, where I have learned so much about what is truly human. He is concerned about the hunters who come up from the big cities to slaughter deer and leave them rotting in the fields. They are only on hand a short while, with their shiny boots and gaudy jackets and their pockets full of money, but they create nothing but noise and havoc. When they finally leave, Bark Point repairs the damage, but each year it is a little worse. In a few more years, Bill fears, Bark Point could become a resort town like Mercer or Eagle River. If it does, he says, he'll move to Canada.

Personally, I don't think we can afford to surrender any more outposts — in our culture and in the remnants of community living that still center around values that make for human dignity. I still say: Let the despoilers feed upon one another. Encourage their self-segregation, away from the mainstream of life. Even give them junk books, if that is all their feeble moments of introspection can bear. But never, *never* surrender.

10

Hope and I

IT WAS only after I had been on television and begun receiving letters from viewers that I realized how seriously interested people are in the personal lives of others. Curiosity about one's immediate neighbors is not intense in a large city. Often you do not see enough of them to get curious. You see more and know more of public figures than of the person in the next apartment. Curiosity about people in public life can become ridiculous when exploited by press agents. But wanting to know more about someone whom you have become interested in as a public personality is as sincere and natural as the wish to know more about the lives of those with whom you have become acquainted in a more personal way.

Still, it was a surprise to me when people wrote to ask who and what I was, where and how I lived, and all about my wife and children. A surprise, but not an affront, for when I receive such letters, I have exactly the same curiosity about those who write them. I really would like to know all about them.

My personal life began on the West Side of Chicago. we lived at 1639 South Central Park Avenue, a neighborhood of houses and trees and good back yards. In our back yard we even had a duck pond with a duck in it, not to mention the flowers and the grass that my father tended so lovingly. My father was a tool and die maker. He could speak and read several languages with ease, had a marvelous sense of humor, and revered greatness. He believed in two things: love and work. He mistrusted those who did not.

Although my father died several years ago, my mother is alive, and now in her late eighties. In the sixty-five years of her life in this country, she has seldom left the kitchen, yet she knows more about the human heart, about human weakness and suffering, and about human caring than I shall ever know. She is gentle and kind, and her adage to me since childhood has been: Keep out of mischief — as sound a bit of wisdom concerning conduct as you are likely to find anywhere, not excluding Spinoza.

It was an alive neighborhood, populated by people of mixed origin, although predominantly Jewish. There was plenty of activity on our street: kids practicing on horns, playing fiddles, playing games — mostly baseball and peg and stick. Peg and stick may require a bit of explanation for the present younger generation. To start the game, it is necessary to steal a broom. This is always done with the confident expectation that this article is something your mother will never miss. Cut off the handle, so you have a stick about twenty-two inches long. Also cut a seven inch peg. Now go out in the street and with your penknife make a hole in the asphalt. In summer the pitch is tacky, so this is no problem. Stand by the hole and, using the stick as a bat, knock the peg down the street. Then mark the hole by putting the stick in it. Your opponent must now take the peg, wherever it lies, and toss it toward the stick. The place it falls is marked, and, of course, as the turns go around, whoever gets the peg closest to the hole wins the point.

But most of all there was an awful lot of talking — on the streets, on the corner by the delicatessen, and among people sitting on their front porches. Talk . . . and lots of laughter. And there were great good times at home, especially in the evenings when my father told stories of his sojourn in Europe, or his adventures in America, or his day-to-day experiences at work.

I was the youngest child in a family of six children, and my life revolved around such matters as dogs, reading, and poetry. I had my own dog, but I also caught every stray dog in the neighborhood, washed and defleaed it, and anointed it with cologne (causing a great rumpus when discovered by one of my sisters from whom the cheap scent had been appropriated). My poetical labors were not properly appreciated by my sisters, either, who would collapse into gales of laughter when I interrupted their bathroom sessions of beauty culture to read them my latest verses.

My father built me a study in the basement and I set up a program of studies for myself: chemistry one week, physics the next, then mathematics, philosophy, etc. It was a wonderful thing until I blew the place up in the course of my chemical experiments. This ended my career in the physical sciences.

One summer I painted our house — a complete exterior paint job utilizing only a one and one-half inch brush. It took me from June to September, and finally the neighbors were complaining to my mother about the way she was working me. They didn't know that I was in no hurry to finish the job. It was not only a labor of love so far as the painting went, but I was spending my time up there in a glory of memorizing poetry and delivering noble dissertations.

I was seldom seen without a book, and nobody regarded this as particularly odd, for the sight of young people reading on the streets, on their porches, on a favorite bench in Douglas Park was common. It is not common today. The only wonder is that I never toppled off a curb or got killed crossing a street — one read as he walked and paid little attention to the hazards of city living.

Furthermore, nobody told us, in school or elsewhere, what a child between the ages of nine and twelve should be reading and what he should read from twelve to fourteen, etc. We read everything that took our fancy, whether we understood it or not, from Nick Carter to Kant and *Penrod and Sam* to Joyce. And when we became infatuated with some writer, we stopped barely short of total impersonation. When I read that Shelley had carried crumbs in his pocket, I started to do likewise and practically lived on breadcrumbs for days.

All of us who grew up in the Depression years on the West Side remember vividly the men out of work and the soup kitchens going on Ogden Avenue; houses and apartments becoming crowded as married sons and daughters moved in with their families. People stayed home and listened to the radio: Wayne King playing sweet music from the Aragon Ballroom and Eddie Cantor singing that potatoes are cheaper, so now's the time to fall in love.

I went to school with the heels worn off my shoes and sat in class with my overcoat on because there were two holes in the seat of my pants. When the teacher asked a question, I would reply with a sermon. I spent my days fuming . . . I hadn't found myself. One day I encountered the works of Schopenhauer and felt I had at last arrived at an idea of life on a highly negative plane. A short time later I presented my whole schema to a friend, who blew it up completely.

My formal education was quite diverse. I never went to school without working to foot the bill and in the course of time did about everything, it seems, except selling shoes. I was an usher at the Chicago Theatre (a vast, gaudy temple of entertainment then featuring elaborate stage shows as well as the latest movies), where I eventually became Chief of Service. I was an errand boy and a newspaper boy (selling papers on the corner of Wabash and Van Buren for a dollar a night, seven o'clock to midnight). I worked in a grocery store, a hardware store, a department store. I was a bus boy and a dishwasher. I sold men's clothing, worked at the University of Chicago, and wrote squibs for a neighborhood newspaper. I went to Crane Junior College, to the old Lewis Institute, and attended graduate courses at the University of Chicago. And during all this, I took courses in every field that captured my imagination or provoked my curiosity: neurol-

ogy, philosophy, psychology, literature, sociology, anthropology, languages (German, especially) . . . everything.

One day, while I was still an undergraduate, a professor whose heart I had captured through my ability to
recite from memory the *Ode to the West Wind*, took me
aside and assured me that if I were to be a teacher of literature, which he suspected would be my goal in life, a
faculty position in a college or university English department was not likely to come easily to a man named Brodsky. Frankly, it was his suggestion that Stuart Brodsky
find another last name — at least if he wanted to become
an English teacher. "What name?" I said. "Any other
name that seems to fit," he replied.

I took the suggestion up with my sisters. We thought
Brent might do nicely. Then I asked my father for his
opinion. He told me that no matter what I did with my
name, I would still be his son and be loved no less. It was
settled. At the age of nineteen, my name was legally
changed to Brent.

Brent or Brodsky, I taught incipient teachers at the
Chicago Teachers College. Then I lectured on Literary
Ideas at the University of Chicago's downtown division.
The world took a nasty turn and I left teaching to enter
the Armed Forces. I spent twenty-seven months in the
army, becoming a Master Sergeant in charge of military
correspondence under Colonel Jack Van Meter. When a
commission was offered me, I asked for OCS training and
got it. But toward graduation time, the prospect of
signing up for two more years as a commissioned officer
was too much and I rejected it. The war was over. I was

on my way to the vagaries of civil life and to becoming a
bookseller.

The Seven Stairs was born, grew, died. I found myself
a widower, endeavoring to maintain my sanity and my
household and fighting for commercial survival on Michigan Avenue.

One day in 1956 a tall, pretty redhead named Daphne
Hersey grew tired of her job in one of the dress shops on
Michigan Avenue and came to work for me. She was a
Junior League girl, but a lot else beside. Before I knew
it, we had three Junior Leaguers working in the shop, and
I was wondering whether the shop was going to be swept
away in an aura of sophistication that was incomprehensible to me. But my respect for Daphne and her integrity
remained limitless. And I had no notion of the improb-
able consequences in the offing.

Nothing is easier than saying hello. The day Hope
walked in to chat with Daphne, the world seemed
simple. She and Daphne had attended Westover together.
They had grown up in the same milieu. Daphne introduced Hope to me. I was three years a widower, absorbed
in my problems of family and business. Hope was a young
girl struggling to stay really alive, teaching at North Shore
Country Day School, living in the token independence
of a Near North Side apartment shared with another
girl. We chatted for a moment or two about books, and I
sold her a copy of a more than respectable best-selling
novel, *By Love Possessed*.

Summer was coming. I was intent upon taking my
children up to Bark Point. I would spend a week or ten

days with them, leave them there with the maid and return for two weeks in the city. Then back again to the
Lake. This was my summer routine. But Daphne wanted
a vacation, too, and we were short of help. While we were
discussing this dilemma, in walked Hope. Daphne asked
her what she was doing during her vacation from kinder-
garten teaching. Nothing. And would she like to work
here for three weeks? Hope accepted. The next day I
left for the Lake. When I returned, Daphne would leave,
and by that time Hope would have learned her way
around. Together with our other girl in the shop, we
could hold the fort until Daphne came back. It was as
simple as that.

When, in due time, I returned, Daphne left and Hope
and I were thrown pretty much together. I loved working with her, and she seemed thrilled with the bookstore.
It was a courtship almost unaware, then a falling in love
with all our might. And the probability of a good outcome seemed almost negligible.

There *is* such a thing as "society." It is not a clique or
gilded salon of arts and letters such as a Lionel Blitzsten
might assemble, but an ingrown family, far more tribal
than what is left of Judaism. In point of fact, the old West
Side no longer exists — its children, our family among
them, are scattered to the winds. But the North Shore,
beleaguered perhaps, is still an outpost of the fair families
of early entrepreneurs, a progeny of much grace anchored
to indescribable taboos.

The plain fact is, it calls for an act of consummate
heroism to withstand real hostility from one's family. It

is not only a matter of the ties of love. It is a matter of who you are, finding and preserving this "who" . . . and you may lose it utterly if you deny your family, just as you may lose it also by failing to break the bonds of childhood.

Even when people try to be understanding and decent, they can be tripped by their vocabulary. In the protective and highly specialized environment in which Hope was raised, anti-Semitism was as much a matter of vocabulary as of practical experience. Even the mild jibes of pet names often involved reference to purported Jewish traits. This atmosphere is so total that those who breathe it scarcely think about it.

This beautiful and vital girl with whom my heart had become so deeply involved, brilliant and well-educated, loved and admired by family and friends, could not possibly make the break that our relationship would call for without the most terrible kind of struggle. Hope's parents were dead, but she had an aunt and uncle and a sister and brother. Their reaction to my impending descent upon their world was one of violent shock and bitter protest.

Hope's relatives were vitally concerned about what she was getting herself into. As if I wasn't! I think if they had pointed out to her that, in addition to being Jewish, I had three small children, that there was an age difference involved, and that she herself might be running away from some nameless fear, they would have stood a better chance of prevailing. But the social impossibility of the case seemed to be the overwhelming obstacle.

If it were all really a dreadful error, I could only pray

that Hope might be convinced of it. I was afraid of marriage. I couldn't afford a love that was not meant to be. I had to think not only of Hope and me, but of the children — they couldn't be subjected to another tragedy. There mustn't be a mistake.

To me, it was a terrible thing to have to remain passive, to ask Hope to shoulder the whole burden of our relationship. We sought out a psychoanalyst to help us — one I had never met socially or in a business way (not easy; I knew nearly all of them on a first name basis) and who, if at all possible, was not Jewish. I did find such a man and Hope arranged to see him. He gave her the facts about the risks involved in marrying me. He also gave assurance that she was neither neurotic nor in need of analysis. And that threw the whole thing right back to Hope again.

Hope left the city to hold counsel with herself. I stayed and did likewise, on the crossroads of my own experience. We had a hard time of it . . . and love won through, feeding, obviously, on struggle, obstacles, impossibilities, and growing all the better for it.

I am sure God was beside me when I married Hope. Since then, everything I do seems right and good. We do everything together . . . my life is empty when she is gone even for a few days. Hope's brother and sister have learned that the "impossible" thing, social acceptance, does not interest me, but that there are other areas of living equally important. We are friends.

Life with love is not without struggle. The struggle is continuous, but so is our love for each other and our family. With the addition of Amy Rebecca, Lisa Jane, and Joseph Peter, the Brent children now number six. It gives us much quiet amusement to hear parents complaining about the difficulties of raising two or three. Hope is responsible for naming Joseph Peter, our youngest. "He looks so much like you and your family," she said, "I think it would be very wrong if we didn't name him after your father." And so we did.

11

My Affair with the Monster

Among the things I have never planned to be, a television performer ranks pretty high on the list.

I have already mentioned that the unlikely person who initiated my relationship with the new Monster of the Age was the wise and kindly Ben Kartman. Ben by this time had left *Coronet Magazine* and was free lancing in editorial and public relations work. I had not seen him for some months when he came into the shop with a public relations man named Max Cooper. Except for having heard of instances in which they purportedly exercised a dangerous power over gossip columnists, I knew nothing about PR boys. I simply regarded them as suspect. Consequently I should probably have taken a dim view of the idea they came in to talk with me about — auditioning for a television program — even if I hadn't been opposed on principle to television.

At the time, it seemed to me that television was the most vicious technological influence to which humanity had been subjected since the automobile's destruction of the art of courtship as well as the meaning of the home. The novelty of TV had not yet worn off, and it was still a shock to walk into a living room and see a whole family sitting before this menacing toy, silent and in semi-darkness, never daring to utter a word while watching the catsup run in some Western killing. I vowed that I would never own a piece of apparatus which seemed so obviously designed to diminish the image of man, enslave his emotions, destroy his incentive, wreck his curiosity, and contribute to total mental and moral atrophy. I didn't think it would be good for the book business, either.

Ben and Max didn't sell me on television, but they did make the audition seem a challenge. What could I do? I had never taken a lesson in acting or public speaking in my life. When I spoke extemporaneously, I often rambled. In fact, that was my approach to talking and to teaching. Sticking to the subject never bothered me . . . or breaking the rules; I didn't know any of them. I just talked. All I had was a spontaneity springing from a love of ideas and of people. I laid these cards on the table as carefully as I could, but Cooper's only response was, "You are a raw talent. I'm sure you can make it."

Make what? On the morning of the auditions, I arrived at the Civic Theatre (an adjunct to the Chicago Civic Opera House which at that time had been taken over as a television studio — this was while Chicago was still active in the game of creating for the medium) and I was as nervous as a debutante on the threshold of her debut. A hundred men and women were standing in the wings, and the fact that I knew some of them and had sold them books made matters worse. All at once, I knew that I was at war with them all. I was competing for a role and I had to be better than the rest.

We were instructed to come out on the stage at a given signal, peer toward a camera marked by two red eyes, and talk, sing, dance, or perform in our fashion for three minutes. By the time my turn came up, I was ready to fall on my face from sheer nervous exhaustion. The red lights blinked on, and I began to talk. I talked for three minutes and was waved off.

I had had enough lecture experience to feel the incompleteness of such an experience. No audience, no response, no nothing, just: your three minutes are up (after all the tension and readiness to go out and perform). I hurried out of the theatre and back to the store, where I paced around like a wild beast. I was certain that I had failed. Everything that I had been building up for seemed cut out from under me, and I could only talk to people or wrap their packages in a mechanical daze.

At five o'clock in the afternoon the spell was broken. Max came in along with a towering young man of massive build who extended a huge hand toward me, crying, "Let me be the very first to congratulate you. You have a television program for the next thirteen weeks!"

At my total astonishment, he threw back his head and emitted a Tarzan laugh. I liked him very much, but I could not place him at all. He was Albert Dekker, an actor who has probably appeared in more Western movies than any other star and who at that time was acting in a

play in Chicago. He was a friend of Cooper's and subsequently a friend of mine, frequently accompanying me
to the television studio during the remainder of his run
in Chicago.

But at that moment I could only sputter and stutter
and wheel around as though preparing for a flying leap,
and the next few minutes gave way to complete pandemonium, as everyone shared in my sudden good fortune.

The show ran for more than thirteen weeks. It lasted a
year. It was sandwiched between a show about nursing
and one about cooking. It was a fifteen minute slot, but in
the course of this time I had to do three commercials —
opening refrigerators and going into the wonders thereof,
selling cosmetics, even houses. It was a mess. During the
entire year, nobody ever evinced any interest in building
the show, and when it was finally cancelled, I was torn
between hurt pride and recognition of an obvious god-
send. Now and then I had received a small amount of
critical acclaim, but on the whole, my first venture into
television seemed a disaster, financially as well as spirit-
ually. And I hate failure.

Well, there was no use apologizing. I had had my
chance, a whole year of it, and I didn't make the grade.
The poor time slot, the overloading of commercials were
no excuse. I could lick my wounds and say, "Nothing
lasts forever. Television is television. They squeeze you
out and throw you out." But in my heart I knew that the
show had never had an audience because it was not good
enough. So it ended in failure, and along with it, my relations with Max Cooper.

For two years, I was away from television entirely, except for an occasional call from Dan Schuffman of WBKB asking me to pinch hit for someone who was taken ill. Among those for whom I served as proxy was Tom Duggan, a real good guy who developed considerable local fame by getting into one scrap after another and finally, after getting into the biggest scrap of all, practically being deported from Chicago to pursue the same career in Southern California where he continues to be a nightly success.

Although it seemed to me from time to time that glimmerings of creativity could be detected in the television field, I no longer had any serious interest in the medium. When, shortly after Hope and I were married, we gave an autographing party for Walter Schimmer, a local TV and radio producer who had written a book called, *What Have You Done for Me Lately?*, the TV relationship was incidental to the objective of boosting a Chicago writer. One of the guests at the party was the station chief of WBKB, Sterling (Red) Quinlan. I had previously met him only casually and was surprised to be drawn into a literary conversation with him, during which he told me that he was working on a book, to be called, *The Merger*. The next day, he sent me the manuscript to read and I found it most interesting, particularly as it dealt with a phase in the development of the broadcasting industry, about which Quinlan, as an American Broadcasting Company vice president, obviously knew a great deal. This was a period during which any number of novels with a background of Big Business were being published. I thought Quinlan had done an unusually honest job with it and wrote him a note to this effect when I returned the manuscript.

Several weeks later, I received a phone call from Quinlan which sounded quite different from the tough-minded executive of my superficial acquaintance. "What's wrong with my book?" he said. "No one wants to publish it." He really wanted to know where he had gone wrong.

I tried to explain the vagaries of publishing and of publishers' tastes and how it was a matter of timing and placement with certain publishers who publish certain types of things. But I could see this made little sense to Quinlan, because there is really not much sense *in* it. Finally I said, "Look, send the book over. You need a front runner. Maybe I can break down a door for you." I'm sure he didn't believe me, but he sent the book over anyway.

I sent the manuscript to Ken McCormick, editor-in-chief at Doubleday, after phoning to tell him about it, and as luck would have it, Ken liked the book and made an offer. I'm sure Quinlan thought I was some kind of wizard, and of course I was delighted to have been able to help.

With Red's book in the process of being published, I turned my mind to other matters — mostly the sheer joy of living. Business was strong, Hope and I were enjoying the best of good times, we were soon to have a child, we were floating on a cloud and wanted no interference from anything. I avoided phone calls and invitations and put away all thoughts of becoming anything in the public eye. I just wanted to be a good bookseller, earn a living, spend time with my family, and leave the world alone.

It was in this frame of mind that I received a call one day from Quinlan asking me to join him for lunch at the Tavern Club (a businessmen's luncheon club located near the WBKB studios). I was interested in Red's literary ambitions and was glad to accept.

Red Quinlan is more than a typical example of a "pulled up by my own boot straps" success story. He is a fairly tall man with reddish hair, a white, smooth face, and blue eyes that can change from pure murder to the softness that only Irish eyes can take on. He knows every way to survive the jungle and moves with the slightly spread foot and duck walk of a man treading a world built on sand. One part of his mind deals only with business; the other part is dedicated to a sensitive appreciation of the written word and a consuming desire to write a good book. At the beginning he may have wanted to make the best seller list, but his concern is now with truth and craftsmanship and with what it means to be a writer. He is a fascinating man who has done much for me.

Two other men joined us for lunch at the club. One was a heavy-set man of Greek descent named Peter DeMet who controlled large interests in the television world. The other was Matt Veracker, general manager of WBKB. We ate a good lunch and talked in generalities until Quinlan asked me if I had read any good books lately. I had just finished a collection of short stories by

Albert Camus and was particularly taken by a piece called, "Artist at Work." As I told the story, DeMet seemed suddenly very interested. But the conversation went no further. We shook hands all around and broke up.

Less than an hour later, Quinlan called me at the shop and asked me to come right over to his office. I could tell as I walked in that something was on the fire. Red came around the desk and sat down with me on the couch. "Stuart," he said, "we have an open half hour following a new science show that the University of Chicago is sponsoring. How would you like to have it?" This was in 1958 when astrophysics had burst upon the public consciousness. Hence the science show.

"I've even thought of the name for your show," Quinlan continued. "Books and Brent."

I still remained silent, caught in an enormous conflict. I *did* want the show . . . to prove something to myself. But at the same time I didn't want to be bothered, I didn't want to get caught up in the hours of study the job entailed. And I no longer needed the money or a listing in the local TV guides to bolster my ego. Yet I wanted the chance again.

Red noted my hesitation and, although slightly nettled by my lack of enthusiasm, recognized that I was not giving him a come-on. He went to the phone and said, "Ask Dan Schuffman to step in here."

Danny took over the argument. The price was set, with promise of a raise within twelve weeks. The show would run from September through June, no cancellation clause,

no commercials sandwiched in to break up the continuity of my presentation. I had complete control over
the choice of books and what I would say about them.
Everything was settled. Now all I had to do was tell
Hope!

It wasn't easy. Hope knew something was on my mind
and refrained from asking about it until the children were
in bed. Then I told my story. It would be five days a
week at the frightening hour of eight o'clock in the morning. Hope took the whole thing in and accepted the situation. But we both had strong misgivings.

I went to work. Each book had to be read and pon-
dered the night before I reviewed it. Asking myself of
each volume what in essence it was really about, what
meanings and values it pointed to, was the crux of the
matter and a most difficult undertaking. Every morning I delivered my presentation and then ran to the bookstore. I came home at six, had dinner, and started preparing for the next morning. It was impossible to entertain
or to see friends, and I was half dead from lack of sleep.
Finally, to lessen the strain of five shows a week, Red
suggested that Hope appear with me on the Friday shows
for a question and answer session, cutting the formal reviews to four a week. Again it took some persuading —
Hope would have nothing to do with it unless she
"looked" right, "sounded" right, and could offer questions
that were sincere and significant. She did all of these
things superbly and for the next three years appeared
with me every Friday.

Still, it was a grueling task. I wanted to give the very

best I could each day, and I felt that I was being drained. But what was really killing my drive was the suspicion that I was working in a vacuum. After all, who could be viewing my dissertations on the problems of man and the universe at eight in the morning? I decided it would probably be appreciated all around if I quit like a gentleman. So one morning, after about eight weeks of giving my all to what I judged to be a totally imaginary audience, I interupted whatever I was talking about and said, "You know, I don't think anyone is watching this program. I'm very tired of peering into two red eyes and talking books just for the sake of talking. I believe I'll quit."

What I really meant to say, of course, was, "If anyone is watching, won't he please drop me a note and say so." But it didn't come out that way. I walked out of the studio thinking it was all over.

To my great astonishment, Quinlan soon reached me by phone at the shop, saying, "What are you trying to do? Get me killed? The phone has been ringing here all morning with people demanding to know why I'm firing you! Did you say that on the air?"

I hastened to explain and told him what I did say. The following day hundreds of letters arrived. I suddenly realized that I had an audience.

Hope and I were thrilled and went to work with renewed vigor. The mail continued to grow. At eight a.m. people were viewing and listening and, of all things, writing to me — not only housewives, but also teachers, librarians, doctors, lawyers, occasional ministers. Newspaper columnists became interested and reviews were flattering to a point where I was afraid I might begin to take myself seriously.

Another thing was also happening. Although I never mentioned on the air that I had a bookstore, people began to call the store asking for books I had reviewed. Other bookstores found that Books and Brent was stimulating their business, and some of them, particularly in outlying areas, took it upon themselves to write notes to the publishers about what was happening. I began to wonder if what the book business needed generally wasn't a coast to coast TV bookshow.

Not long after these thoughts had formed in my mind, Pete DeMet asked me to come and see him at the hotel where he was staying. When I arrived, I found his room filled with men . . . some kind of important meeting was just breaking up. Finally they dispersed and I was able to sit down with Pete. He told me he wanted to create a TV book of the month show, which he was ready to back to the hilt. He would investigate the possibility of getting the major publishers to pay for some of the time — the rest would be sold to other sponsors. Apparently he and his organization had the genius required to market such a thing. In any event, his gospel was "success" and he evidently saw in me another way to be successful.

I always had mixed reactions to this powerful, heavy-faced man with his white silk shirts and his, to me, mysterious world of promotional enterprise. He had been in the automobile business and subsequently acquired ownership of successful network shows, particularly in the sports field, and no one seemed to doubt that he could do anything he set his mind to.

He was always forthright in his relations with me. He boasted that he had never read a book and never intended to, but he saw in my work a vision of something he wanted to be part of. But he also insisted: "If I take you on, I own you."

Contracts were being drawn up, but Hope and I decided that although the amount of money being offered me — $130,000 for nine months of work — seemed extraordinary, the only thing to do was to turn the offer down.

So I went to see Pete and told him the deal was off. The money was wonderful, but so was my marriage, my personal life. I couldn't see myself catching a plane to the West Coast on a moment's notice, only to be told that I was heading for the East Coast the following week. There might be some excitement in such a frenetic pace, but I was getting too old for that sort of thing, and I didn't need the pace and the noise to persuade me that I was living.

My would-be benefactor looked at me as though I had gone out of his mind, but he let me go without any further badgering.

By this time I had become more than a little intrigued with the Frank Buck approach to capturing live talent. On the next occasion DeMet pressed me to sign the contract, he assured me that I wasn't nearly as good or important as I thought I was. They were not at all certain, he said, of my "acceptance" in various markets, and fur-

thermore there was threat now of replacing me altogether: some people felt that a Clifton Fadiman or a Vincent Price with a "ready-made" or "built-in" audience
would be distinctly preferable to someone completely
unknown outside of Chicago. It would take a lot of adroit
PR work to build up the ratings for an unknown.

I couldn't contradict him, and happily I did not feel
smart-alecky enough to tell him, "Go ahead and get those
fellows if you think they can bring a book to life better
than I can." I simply refused to sign without the consent
of my wife.

That night I was in the midst of reporting the day's
events to Hope when the phone rang. Hope answered.
It was for me: Pete saying, "Can I come over? I *must* see
you now."

A half hour later Pete was with us, going through the
entire proposition and concluding by saying, "You'll do
everything I tell you to do, and you'll make a fortune.
We'll all make money."

Hope looked Mr. DeMet squarely in the eyes and said,
"Money isn't the God of this household and at the moment
I can't say I enjoy being here with you."

In the stunned silence that followed, I was seized with
a feeling of terrible embarrassment over our attacking
Pete DeMet on a level so totally removed from his frame
of reference or the very principles of his existence. A
few minutes later, Pete got his hat and left. I was sure
the whole thing was finished.

As it happened, it was just the beginning. One of our
best friends, in or out of television, was the late Beuhlah

Zackary, producer of "Kukla, Fran and Ollie" and as fine
a spirit as I have ever known. She used to say to me, "If
I can only discover exactly what makes you tick, I'll
make you a household name throughout the nation."
Had she lived, I'm convinced she would have done it. In
any event, it was Beuhlah at this point who saw merit
lurking somewhere beneath the high pressure and convinced Hope and me that we should explore the matter
further. Finally we consented to go ahead, provided Jack
Pritzker act as our attorney and read every line of every
paper (including the dotting of i's and the crossing of t's)
before it was signed. Things were agreed upon to everyone's satisfaction, and I was in the Pete DeMet organization.

I had confided in Hardwick Moseley at Houghton
Mifflin about the enterprise and he wrote to me (in
March of 1959): "I do hope the DeMet deal on Books
and Brent goes through and that you get your rightful
share of the plunder. You know I always expected something like this. I am delighted that it is happening so
soon. When you get time why not let me know a little of
the detail. If we can get you on in the high grass and a
variety of stations everywhere it will be the best thing
that has happened to the book business in years because
you do sell books."

It seemed a long time since Hardwick had lifted me
from the depths by writing me that I *had* to remain a
bookseller, no matter what.

But everything fell through from the very beginning.
The money Pete hoped to raise from the publishing indus-

try failed to materialize at all. Television does not sell books, the publishers chorused. From my end, I was assailed by doubts because I was never invited to present the proposition to the publishers with whom I was most intimately acquainted. From Pete's end, there was anger and frustration when the industry would not buy something which he was convinced might prove their economic salvation. He decided to look for other markets.

Production was scheduled to start in September. But by this time other things had taken precedence over Books and Brent. Pete entered into a real estate promotion to develop a kind of Disney wonderland in New York called Freedom Land. His lawyer, Milt Raynor, wrote to me in flattering terms about myself and the book project, but indicated that for the time being the undertaking would have to be shelved.

It was a letdown. But the irony of the thing was that a promotional genius like Pete could be so fascinated by the publishing field and what might be done for it, and then so totally discouraged by the supineness, invincible ignorance, and general reluctance of an enormous, potentially very profitable industry to take even modest advantage of the only advertising medium that might bring it before the public. Pete found only one publisher actively encouraging. The rest were negative.

This was the idea they were offered: I was to review, on a network show, books selected by myself from the lists of all publishers. In our experience in Chicago, although I rarely, if ever, suggested that anyone rush down to his neighborhood bookstore (if any) and buy the book in question, every bookstore in the area felt the impact of my lectures. The instances in which my own store sold hundreds of books in a week because of a review I had given were fantastic — and more frequently than not the very large downtown stores considerably outsold my own shop on the same volume, for I was not engaged in self-advertising. This is something unique in our day, but not in publishing experience, for Alexander Woollcott used to have the same effect through his radio broadcasts. He was, of course, a national figure . . . but not in a popular sense until he went on the radio. Publishers were aware of all this, but they were not convinced.

Pete was convinced. He believed in me because he saw the results of the job I was doing in a very difficult city and saw no obstacle to doing at least as much in other cities. He was an entrepreneur, but perfectly willing to try the idea of wedding television to culture. Actually, I was never a party to any of the planning, any of the strategy, any of the meetings held with publishers or their representatives. To this day, I know nothing of what actually went on. I was just the talent, and all I knew was that there was a clause in the contract that required Pete to put the show on the road no later than September 30, 1959, or else I was free to return to my local television commitments. The option was not picked up, and that was that.

As I mulled the whole thing over at Bark Point, a comment of my father's kept running through my mind: "When is a man a man? Only when he can stand up to his bad luck."

Of course, there was no saying whether the luck was really bad — only that what I envisioned for the future was certainly being held in abeyance. I came back for another year of Chicago television, much like the year before, except for the feeling that I was bringing more experience to it.

It was the letters that kept me persuaded I was right. In spite of the hour, with wives kissing husbands off to work and mothers frantically preparing breakfast and dressing children for school, people were listening and, in increasing number, writing. Greater numbers of people were searching for answers to forgotten questions, or driven, perhaps, back to fundamental questions and to restating them. Hope and I found all this mail a tremendous stimulus. We returned to our city routine. Every evening I came home from the bookstore, had dinner, played or talked with the children, then sat down to read, while Hope read or knitted or mended or listened to music. At midnight we took a short walk to the corner drugstore with Mr. Toast, our Golden Retriever, and had a cup of hot chocolate. These moments were the best of the whole day.

Getting to the studio in the morning was never easy, and on Fridays when we made the mad rush together it was more than usually frantic. Hope is not easy to awaken and would be engaged, more often than not, as we raced across the street like maniacs toward our parked car, in the final acts of dressing, zipping up her skirt, straightening her hair, trying to find her lipstick. Sometimes we barely made it ahead of the cancellation period — five minutes before showtime, but we always

managed. Then when the ordeal was over, it was perfectly delicious to go out for coffee, swearing solemnly,
absolutely, never again would we oversleep . . . until
the next time.

But why were we doing it? The financial rewards for
an unsponsored, sustaining program simply bore no relation whatever to the effort involved. Finally Quinlan
called me in and suggested that since the networks didn't
seem interested, it might be a good idea to form an organization and see if I couldn't sell the show myself.

Hy Abrams, my lawyer and tennis partner, and his
brother-in-law, David Linn, often used to ask why I didn't
do anything about promoting the show, to which my answer normally was: "Do what?" But now, with Red's in-
sistence, I had a feeling that perhaps the time was ripe.
Perhaps in the present era of political, economic, and
spiritual confusion, people might be becoming worried,
harassed, clipped, chipped, agonized enough for a return to reading. They might be susceptible.

David was all for it, and we called a meeting, bringing
together, as I recall, Ira Blitzsten, Sidney Morris, Adolph
Werthheimer, and my brother-in-law, Milton Gilbert. I
made the presentation, outlining not only the prospect
but also the likelihood of absolute failure. Together we
created the Stuart Brent Enterprises and hired a man to
run the show. Again the idea was to sell the thing to the
publishing industry. The project hardly got off the
ground, yet our case seemed an extremely sound one.

To begin with, we surveyed a thousand letters that had
been written to the Books and Brent show. A summary
of the survey showed:

Of the 1000 letters read, 705 or 70.5% had bought one or more books due to Stuart's review. Some writers had bought as many as ten books. Many listed the books bought and several enclosed sales slips.

Of the 1000 letters read, 107 or 10.7% planned to buy in the near future. Many of these pointed out the difficulties of buying books in the suburbs, where there are few bookstores.

Of the 1000 letters read, 188 or 18.8% wrote "keep up the good work" type of letters. There were requests for book lists, particularly from librarians. A number suggested starting a book club.

Libraries, bookstores, and publishers were represented. The letters showed a good cross section of the community, both economically and age-wise.

David Lande, of Brason Associates, a distributing agency for publishers, helped the cause by writing to Mac Albert, of Simon and Schuster, a letter that said: "While this may not be news to you, I thought you might be interested in knowing that the Stuart Brent book review program has caught on like 'wildfire' in this area. Our personal experience has been that Stuart Brent has made more best sellers than Jack Paar. If this is good information for you, use it — if not, we're still good friends."

I went to New York and had an opportunity to talk with Mr. Simon, of Simon and Schuster, along with other editors, publishers, and booksellers. Mr. Simon said, "I like you because you are not interested in the I.Q. of man, but in his C.Q."

"What, sir," I said, "is the C.Q.?"

"His cultural quotient," he replied. Then he said: "The book business is exploding. We have a lot of new schools, a lot of new libraries. So long as we believe that a child must attend school until eighteen years of age, we will need a great many textbooks. People are hungry for a lot of new things. Books are one way of appeasing that new hunger. No matter where you go or how small the community, you will usually find a new library building and new schools. The book business has a new, great future. We need more good writers to fill the need for books these days. That's our problem, finding new writers, good writers."

Most of the major New York publishers and some of the smaller ones bought time on Books and Brent to help initiate its showing on WOR-TV. The pre-taped half-hour shows made their debut simultaneously in New York and Los Angeles on September 12, 1960. In the October 26 issue of *Variety*, the showbusiness weekly, Thyra Samter Winslow said: "The best of the new live shows is certainly Stuart Brent, who reviews books, and books only, daily Monday through Friday, on WOR-TV. . . . His style is easy, intimate, calm, interesting. Who knows? He may give just the fillip needed to cause a renaissance of reading by the home girls. And about time, too!"

In Chicago, Paul Molloy, the *Sun-Times* columnist, who had followed this apparent breakthrough with great enthusiasm, commented on the record of 2,700 letters received during the first four weeks of the broadcasts. "More interesting," he said, "than the plaudits, however, is the fact that Brent went out on his own and sold the show because he's convinced there's a market for it. Most broadcasters aren't, but they'll have to come around to it. For 2,700 letters in four weeks is a lot of reaction. Even The Untouchables doesn't touch this record. For my part, I find Brent the most scholarly and at the same time most down to earth teletalker in Chicago today. I've yet to leave one of his shows without having learned — or at least thought — something."

But in spite of all the good sendoffs, TV syndication of Books and Brent failed to pick up the additional sponsorship necessary to make it a going concern. Hal Phillips, program director of KHJ-TV in Los Angeles, wrote: "After much discussion and consideration, we have determined that we will not be continuing with the 'Books and Brent' series after Friday, December 2, 1960. This in no way reflects upon our feeling of the top quality and standard of the program. The decision is based upon the lack of sales potential, etc. We have liked this series and have had fine viewer response from it and regret that we will have to discontinue these programs."

This time, when my venture crumbled, I did not feel affected too deeply. I continued with my daily broadcasts from WBKB, fully prepared to accept their demise also. By this time I had a realistic sense of the pressures to which this industry is subject, and I knew this was a world in which I could not afford to get involved. At the end of my third successive year, the rumors began to circulate. Then Danny Schuffman dropped a hint at lunch one day. Danny has been carefully schooled in the diplomacy of the television jungle and unless you were listening with a third ear you would probably never catch the veiled meaning of the innocent remark.

After all, while nobody questioned the public service value of the show, the fact remained that the "rating" was at a standstill and there was apparently no possibility of getting a sponsor. At the same time that an estimated 20,000 were viewing me, 46,000 were supposed to be watching something on another channel, 61,000 on another, and 70,000 on still another. The competition must be met. The parent company in New York wants higher ratings. The stockholders want higher profits. Five days a week is too much exposure anyway. Books and Brent has had it. In a world about equally divided between those who are scared to death and those too bored to do anything anyway, the soundness of these operational judgments can scarcely be questioned.

When, finally, Red Quinlan got around to telling me all about this, I knew what was coming and offered no objections. It would have been inconceivable for us to part except as friends. And my mild, husbandly trepidation about breaking the news to Hope proved utterly groundless. She was simply delighted.

During the last weeks of my daily broadcasts, I planned every show with the greatest care and instead of reviewing new and popular fiction and non-fiction, I chose the most profound works that I felt capable of dealing with. In succession, I talked on Mann's *The Magic Mountain*, Proust's *Remembrance of Things Past*, Joyce's *Ulysses*, Kafka's *The Trial*, Camus' *The Stranger*, Galsworthy's short story, *Quality*, Northrop's *Philosophical Anthropology*, Hemingway's *The Old Man and the Sea*, *Hamlet*, *Job*, *Faust*, and *Peer Gynt*, Fromm's *The Art of Loving*,

Erickson's *Childhood and Society*, Huxley's *Brave New World*, Dostoevski's *Crime and Punishment; Four Modern American Writers*, and Stendahl's *The Red and the Black*. It was a pretty wild course in Western literature and the results were astounding, not only in viewer response, but also in the run on these books experienced by bookstores throughout the city and the suburbs.

Demand was particularly sensational for Father du Chardin's *The Phenomena of Man*, also included in this series. A check of bookstores in the area showed sales or orders of approximately 900 copies in a single day. Over 2300 copies of this one title were sold in less than one month. Our shop sold almost 600 copies. A. C. McClurg's reported: "We had 375 copies of *Phenomena of Man* on hand before Brent's review. By 3:30 that afternoon we sold them all and wired Harper and Brothers for 500 more." McClurg's had moved only 150 copies of the book during the previous five months.

When I reviewed *The Red and the Black*, we had only ten copies in stock at the shop (in the Modern Library edition) and sold them out immediately. We tried picking up more from McClurg's, but they too were sold out. I then called one of the large department store book sections to see how they were doing. The clerk who answered the phone said, "No, we don't have a copy in stock. We're all sold out."

"Was there a run on the book?" I said.

"Yes, as a matter of fact there was."

"Can you tell me the reason?"

"Yes, you see they've just made a movie out of the book."

He almost had me persuaded until I checked the theatres. There was no such movie — not playing Chicago, anyway.

Since I continually counseled men and women to accept life, to live it, to change themselves if necessary, but never to turn against creation or to abandon love and hope, never to fall for the machine or the corporation or to look for Father in their stocks and bonds, I was hardly in a position — even armed with the facts and figures — to try to fight the organization for the saving of Books and Brent. I did, however, two weeks before the series ended, take the audience into my confidence and explain the situation as fairly as I could. Mr. Quinlan had my talk monitored and agreed that I handled the matter with sincerity and truthfulness. There was nothing Red could do — he was tied to an organization that was too impersonal to respond to the concerns of a mere 20,000 people. We understood each other perfectly on this score.

But what happened after my announcement was something neither of us ever expected, even though we knew there were some people out there who bought books and wrote heartwarming letters. Phone calls began coming into the studio by the hundreds, letters by the thousands. One late afternoon, Red called me and said, "I knew you were good, but not that good. I just got a call from the asylum at Manteno protesting your cancellation. Even the madmen like you." We both laughed but we were touched, too.

Letters, telegrams, and even long distance phone calls began to plague the chairman of the board in New York

City. Letters by the score were sent to Mr. Minow in Washington. But the most beautiful letters were those directed to Hope and me, on every kind of paper, written in every kind of hand, some even in foreign languages. Until this has happened to you, it is impossible to imagine the feeling. The meaning of a mass medium strikes you and all at once it seems worthwhile to cope with the whole shabby machinery if you are able to serve through it.

Hope and I sat reading every bit of mail late into the night. She said: "Do you remember telling me what F. Scott Fitzgerald said?" I looked puzzled. "He said that America is a willingness of the heart," she prompted.

I have indicated that Red Quinlan is a man who knows his business and his way around in it, and that he is also a man deeply enamored of the world of letters. He was even less ready than I to call it quits. He invited me to lunch one day, and after pointing out that, anyway, for the sake of my health the five-day-a-week grind was too much of a strain to be continued, he asked, "But how about once a week at a good hour with a sponsor?"

I hesitated. The columnists had broken the story of my demise at WBKB. Another station had shown interest and we had had preliminary talks. But the fact was, I couldn't have asked for better treatment than WBKB had given me. Nobody ever told me what to do or how to slant my program. The crew on the set could not have been more helpful. I felt at home there. And while Hope had at first been concerned about the possibility of our lives being wrecked by the awful demands television exacted, she was now beginning to worry about the people

who wrote in, telling about the needs that my show somehow ministered to. When Red sold the show on a weekly
basis to Magikist, a leading rug cleaning establishment,
there was really no doubt about my decision. When I met
Mr. Gage, the president of the corporation, he said, "If my
ten year old daughter likes you and my wife likes you,
that's enough for me. I'm sure everybody will like you.
And we'll try very hard to help you, too." If you can just
get that kind of sponsor, things become a good deal
easier. But somehow, I do not think the woods are full of
them.

Quinlan's interest in conveying through television some
of the excitement of the world of books and ideas also resulted in an interesting experimental program called
"Sounding Board," in which I was invited to moderate a
panel of literary Chicagoans in a monthly two-hour late-
evening discussion on arts and letters. Our regular panel
consisted of Augie Spectorsky, editor of *Playboy Magazine*; Van Allen Bradley, literary editor of the *Daily
News*; Fannie Butcher, literary editor of the Chicago *Tribune;* Hoke Norris, literary editor of the Chicago *Sun-
Times;* Paul Carroll, then editor of the experimental
literary magazine, *Big Table*; Hugh Duncan, author, and
Dr. Daniel Boorstin, professor of American history at the
University of Chicago. They were fine discussions and we
kept them up for six months, but nobody would pick up
the tab.

My approach to television performance, being untu-
tored, is probably quite unorthodox. I do not work from
notes. In preparation, I first read the book, then think

about it, seeking connective links and related meanings. In the actual review of the book, I quite often stray into asides that assume greater importance than the review it- self.

I never say to myself: this is the theme, this is the mid- dle, this the end. I say: get into the heart of the book and let your mind distill it, and, as often happens, enlightening relationships with other books and ideas may develop.

I cannot perform in a state of lassitude. Before the cameras, I always find myself tightening up until the floor manager signals that I'm ON. For a moment, I am all tenseness, realizing that people are watching me, but in a few minutes I have forgotten this and am thinking about nothing but the book and the ideas I am talking about. Now I am carried by the mood and direction of thought. If I want to stand, I stand; if I want to sit, I sit; if I want to grimace, I grimace. Nothing is rehearsed or calculated in advance. All I can do is unfold a train of thought springing from the study that has preceded performance, and the toll is heavy. Sometimes after the show, I can barely straighten up, or I may be utterly dejected over my inability to say all I should have said. Then I leave the studio, moody and silent.

I never talk to anyone before a show except my direc- tor. He understands me and knows how easily I'm thrown. It can be a slight movement from the boom man or a vari- ation in the countdown signal from the floor manager, something unexpected in the action of a camera man or a slight noise somewhere in the studio, and I react as though someone threw a glass of water in my face. Then I am off the track, floundering like a ship without a rudder. Sometimes I can right myself before the show is ended, sometimes not. Hence the frequent depression, for I feel that every show must be the best show possible, that "off" days are not permitted, and that I can never indulge myself in the attitude of, "Oh well, better one next time." When people are watching and listening, you must perform, and perform your best.

Often my grammar goes haywire. I know better, but I can become helpless against the monster known as time. I have to fight time. I cannot hesitate or make erasures. So I plunge on, hoping that some one significant thought may emerge clearly — some thought perhaps as vital as that which animates the pages of *The Phenomena of Man*, calling on us to recognize the eternal core of faith and courage: Courage to rebel and faith in the realization of our own being. Courage that takes the self seriously; faith that is grounded in activity.

I hesitate to make any predictions about the future of television, as a means of communication or as a business. As a business, it must be run for profit. The argument is not about this point, but about the level of operation from which such profit shall be sought. From personal experience, I can say that TV does not have to constitute a blow to life itself. Perhaps many of us are "mindless in motion" and now sit "mindlessly motionless" in front of our TV sets. But I take heart in the certain knowledge that many men and women are not so much concerned with the camera eye as they are in finding a way back to the inward eye.

12

Life in the Theatre

THERE ARE even odder ways of life than sitting alone behind a desk in a little room lined with books waiting for someone to come in and talk with you, or delivering sermons on literature to the beady red eyes of a television camera. One of them is the theatre.

You may recall the scene in Kafka's *The Trial* in which K meets the Court Painter and goes to this innocuous madman's room, ostensibly to learn more about the Judge who is to sit at the trial. The room is so tiny, K has to stand on the bed while the Painter pulls picture after picture from beneath this lone article of furniture, blows the dust off them into K's face, and sells several to him. Although the reader recognizes from the beginning that it is all a tissue of lies and deception, K leaves feeling satisfied that at last he has someone on his side who will put in a "right" word for him. It is evident to what ends K will now go to bribe, cheat, blackmail, be made a total fool of, in the hope of getting someone to intervene in his fate.

In addition to its comment upon a culture that would rather surrender identity than face up to its guilt, the scene is terribly funny, as well as terribly humiliating.

It is this scene that always comes to mind when I think of the nightmare of nonsense I lived through in the course of three weeks in the theatre. It happened one summer a few years ago when Hope and I had come down from Bark Point to check on the shop. I was answering a pile of letters when the phone rang. It was a man I had met sometime before who turned out to be business manager of a summer stock theatre operating in a suburb northwest of Chicago. He wondered if I would like to play a lead opposite Linda Darnell in the Kaufmann and Hart comedy, *The Royal Family*. The role was that of the theatrical agent, Oscar Wolfe, who theoretically functioned as a sane balance to a family of zany, childish, totally mischievous grown-ups (roughly modeled on the Barrymore clan).

Hope, who had grown up in Westchester society, admitted that when she was a girl attending summer theatre it had always been her secret wish to be a part of it. She thought it might be good fun, even though I had never acted in my life. So the business manager came over and I signed the contract, calling for a week of rehearsal and two weeks of performance.

Summer theatre around Chicago cannot be classified as an amateur undertaking, although part of its economics is based on utilizing large numbers of young people who want the "training" and generally avoiding the high costs involved in regular theatrical production. But top stars and personalities are booked, the shows are promoted to

the public as professional offerings and are reviewed as
such by the theatrical critics, and the whole enterprise is
regarded as essential to the vitality of a "living theatre."
The outfit I signed up with was an established enterprise
and, as a matter of fact, is still going. I was not entirely
confident that I could deliver, but I had no doubt that I
was associating myself with people who could.

The theatre itself was not a refashioned barn or circus
tent set-up, but an actual theatre building, restored from
previous incarnations as a movie and vaudeville house. I
arrived on a lovely August morning but inside the theatre
was in total darkness except for some lights on the stage. I
made my way timidly down front where a number of people were sitting. Several nodded to me, and I nodded
back. Presently a tall man got up on the stage and announced that he was going to direct the play. He said,
however, that Miss Darnell had not yet arrived and, also,
that there were not enough scripts to go around. We
would begin with those who had their parts.

For the next three days, I sat in the darkness from nine
in the morning until five in the afternoon. No one asked
me to read, no one asked me to rehearse, practically no
one talked to me at all. I managed a few words with Miss
Darnell, who was gracious and charming, but I was beginning to wonder when I would be asked to act. Hope had
been working with me on my lines, but it is one thing to
know lines sitting down and quite another to remember
them while trying to act and give them meaning before
an audience.

I began to suspect that something was haywire. A
friend who taught drama at a nearby college and often

took character roles in stock confirmed my fears by assuring me that this play would never get off the ground. "It will never open," he said.

We were to open on a Monday. It was already Friday and I had been on stage exactly once and nobody yet knew his part — I least of all. In addition to my fears, I was beginning to feel slighted. I wondered what I was doing in this dark, dank place, and what the rest thought they were doing, including the innumerable young men and women between sixteen and twenty years of age who were ostensibly developing their knowledge of the theatre through odd jobs such as wardrobe manager, program manager, etc. There didn't seem much to manage and I wasn't sure it was really a very healthy environment. By this time, a fair number of the cast had taken to screaming, which is something I am not used to among grown-ups for any extended period. I also had my doubts about a young man who spent most of his offstage moments sweet-talking a bulldog. I wondered if acting necessarily precluded any kind of emotional responsibility.

Saturday night the play preceding us closed. We rehearsed all that night. Sunday the theatre would be dark, and Monday *The Royal Family* was to go on. The Saturday night rehearsal was initially delayed because one of the principals could not be found. Finally he was located, dead drunk, in a local tavern. It was now almost one a.m. and not even a walk-through with script in hand had yet been attempted. Instead the company was engaged in a welter of screeching, shouting, confusion, and recriminations. This was sheer, silly nonsense I decided, and went to see the business manager. I told him I'd be pleased to quit and offered to pay double my salary to any experienced actor he could get to replace me. I was at once threatened with a lawsuit.

At two in the morning, everyone was called on stage by the director, who made a little speech saying that he was just no longer able to direct the play, he couldn't pull it together! At this, Miss Darnell walked off the stage, saying, "This play will not open on Monday or Tuesday or ever, unless something is done immediately." After all, she had a reputation to uphold.

Thereupon, the director returned with a further announcement. It so happened, he said, that a brilliantly gifted young New York director was "visiting here between important plays" and he had consented to pull the play together for us! Our gift of Providence then stepped forward and we began to rehearse.

When my cue came and I offered my lines, the new director said: "The Oscar Wolfe part is really just an afterthought. The show will play just as well without the Wolfe character appearing at all."

"Fine," I said, but pandemonium had already broken loose as the former director and some of the actors took issue with this new twist. We were already missing one actor and now this new director wanted to sack me. Well, I had asked for it, but Miss Darnell and the others persuaded me to stick with it. The rehearsal continued.

At five a.m. a halt was called and the treasurer of the theatre asked to say a few words. Under Equity rules, he reminded us, we were entitled to overtime for extra rehearsal. He asked us to waive this for the sake of the play. I waited silently to see what the general reaction would be. It didn't take long to find out: Nothing doing, play or no play! I went along with them on that. What I couldn't understand was why they put up with all they did: the filthy little cubicles that served as dressing rooms, the rats and cockroaches that scudded across the floor, the lack of any backstage source of drinking water — the whole atmosphere seemed deliberately designed to make an actor's life completely insupportable. And now the management was sulking because the actors didn't have enough "love for the theatre" to forgo their pay for overtime.

At six a.m. it was decided that rehearsal would resume at one o'clock in the afternoon. As we were about to leave, too tired to care any longer about anything, the director came up and said he was sure I must have misunderstood him. He would indeed be sorry if I left the show or if he had hurt my feelings. What he had really meant to say was that the Oscar Wolfe part lends credence to the movement and meaning of the play. I was glad to leave it at that.

The following afternoon, before evening rehearsals, Hope and I stopped at a drugstore a few steps from the theatre. There we found Miss Darnell sitting in a booth sipping a coke. She motioned us over.

"The play won't open Monday," she said. "I've made my decision."

We agreed wholeheartedly.

"But have you heard the latest?"

"No," we said.

"The play that follows us in is falling apart, too. An old

time actor in it, pretty well known for his paranoia, slugged a young actress for a remark she made and someone else jumped in and put him in the hospital."

"What's next with our show?" I said. "Has a replacement been found for our drunken friend?"

"Yes. He's busy now rehearsing his lines."

"This is a world such as I've never been in," I said. "I've never seen anything like it."

"Neither have I. Not like this one," said Linda Darnell.

On stage, we again worked all night. It was a mess. The director was in a rage. He scowled, threatened, exhorted. Everybody was going to pieces. No one talked to anyone.

On Monday morning, we started at ten, planning to rehearse up to curtain time. But at five in the afternoon, Miss Darnell told the management she would not appear, and under her contract they could do nothing but accept her decision. We went back to work that night and rehearsed until five in the morning.

Came Tuesday afternoon and we were back again in our black hole of Calcutta. By now we were all more than a little hysterical and the language would have been coarse for a smoker party. Some of the players were so exhausted they slept standing up. But now the play was finally getting under way. Zero hour was approaching. The curtain went up and the show began.

Opening night was incredible. In scene after scene, lines were dropped, cues forgotten, and ad libs interjected to a point that it was almost impossible to stay in character. The actress who claimed she had played her part as

an ancient dowager for the last twenty years ("Everywhere — I even played it in Australia") forgot her lines
and was utterly beside herself. She said never had she
been subjected to such humiliation. One actor tripped
over her long morning coat and fell on his face. A bit of a
nut anyway, he got up gracefully, muttered some inanities,
and tickled the old dowager under the chin. She reared
back, nostrils flaring. All this time, I was sitting at a piano
observing the scene, feeling like a somnambulist.

But the play went on, and although it certainly improved during its run, the relations of the cast did not.
Every evening we came in, put on our make-up, and
dressed for our parts without saying a word. One night I
lost a shirt. Another night an actress had her purse stolen.
On another occasion a fist fight broke out between an actor
and an actress. Backstage life went on either in utter silence or in bursts of yelling, screaming, and hair-pulling.
The atmosphere was thick with hostility. But on stage it
was as though nothing outside the world of the play had
ever happened, unless you were close enough to hear
names still being called under the breath. It was crazy.

Many of us in the cast were asked to appear on television interviews to promote the show. A good friend of
mine, Marty Faye, who has had one of the longest continuous runs on Chicago TV, asked me to appear on his
late evening broadcast. Since the gossip columnists in the
city were already having a field day over the strife at this
well-known summer playhouse, I told Marty (and his
viewing audience) my reaction to the affair and to what
I had seen of the theatre in general. I had no idea I was

exploding such a bombshell. From right and left, I was attacked by everyone (including the lady who had had such a horrible experience playing the dowager) as a traitor to the theatre and its great traditions. By everyone, that is, except Miss Darnell and her leading man, who agreed that something might be done for actors if the public knew of the conditions under which they so often work and of the wretched, tragic life they so frequently have to lead. What a terrible waste this amounts to! No wonder you have to be virtually insane to pursue a career in the theatre!

Herb Lyons, the *Tribune* columnist, couldn't stop laughing over lunch the day I told him my experiences. Irv Kupcinet, the *Sun-Times* columnist, however, whose talented daughter was among our struggling players, failed to see any humor in the situation. But the real payoff came when checks were distributed after the first week of our engagement. For the week of rehearsals, I had received the munificent sum of thirty-five dollars, but my salary for actual performance was to be two hundred and fifty dollars per week. My check for the first week's work was $18.53! What happened to the rest of the money? Well, in the first place, I had to join the union and pay six months dues. Then I had to pay the full price for any seats I reserved for friends or relatives and even for a seat for Hope. Then I paid for the daily pressing of my suit and the laundering of my shirts and even a hidden fee for the use of the dressing room. Finally, there was the usual social security and withholding tax deduction.

But the whole Kafka nightmare was well worth it. In

spite of acquiring at least one enemy for life and no monetary profit at all, I gained some friends who take the theatre seriously and in a treacherous business, are determinedly making headway. In addition, Linda Darnell, a person of great sweetness, has become a cherished acquaintance. It is not often one comes out of a nightmare so well.

13

Writing and Publishing

I KNEW she was crazy the moment she entered the room. It was a miserable November day, snowing and blowing, when a woman with a round face, rosy from the bitter cold, wearing a long raincoat and a hat trimmed with big bright cherries burst into the old Seven Stairs and almost ran me into the fireplace.

"Are you Mr. Brent?" she cried. She was fat and dumpy and she now took a deep breath and stood on tiptoe, running the tip of her tongue across her lips.

"I am," I said, backing away behind the desk.

"Oh, Mr. Brent, a friend of yours sent me. I teach her children at the Lab school, and she thinks you're a wonderful man. And now, seeing you, I think so, too!" She breathed deeply again. "I have a wonderful book, a divine book, that will change everything ever written for children. You must be the first to see it. I've brought it along."

With this, she removed the long raincoat and began

peeling off one sweater after another. I remained behind the desk watching the sweaters pile up and thinking, if she attacks me I'll make a break for the stairs and yell for help.

Finally she started to undo a safety pin at one shoulder, then at the other, and then she unbuttoned a belt about her fat waist. These apparently related to some kind of suspension system beneath her dress, for she now pulled forth, with the air of a lunatic conjurer, a package wrapped in silk which she deposited on my desk and began to unwrap ever so delicately. She did have lovely long fingers.

As the unwrapping proceeded, her mood changed from hysterical exuberance to one of command. "Take this cover and hold it," she directed, her lower lip thrust out aggressively. I held the cover while she backed off and unfolded the book, her eyes fixed upon me with a wicked gleam.

"This book shows something no other book has ever dared to do," she said. "It shows the true Christmas Spirit. Look carefully and you'll see the new twist. Instead of showing Santa Claus coming down the chimney, I have shown Santa coming *up* the chimney! Furthermore I'm prepared to make you my agent. I'll work with you day and night. Are you married? No? I thought not. My dear boy, we'll make ecstasy together and be rich!"

It was a delicate situation. I told her I did not think she should let the manuscript out of her hands, but in the meantime I would think of some publisher who might be interested in a new twist about Santa Claus.

Without another word, she wrapped up the book, pinned it back to her stomach, strapped the belt about her, piled one sweater on after the other, put on her hat and raincoat, and backed away like a retreating animal until she hit the door. Then, still staring at me, she slowly turned the knob, flung open the door, and fled into the cold November morning. Her poor soul haunted me for days.

Long before I was known to anyone else, I began to be sought out by people who wanted to write, or had written and wanted to publish, or had even gone to the futile expense of private publication. There was an October night when I was nearly frightened out of my wits, while sitting before the fire at the Seven Stairs, by the sudden appearance of a tall young man with a black hat pulled far down over one eye and a nervous tenseness that warned me immediately of a stick-up. His opening remark, "You're open rather late," didn't help any, either.

I remained uneasy while he looked around. Finally he bought two records and a volume of poetry, but he seemed loath to leave. He had a rather military bearing and handsome, regular features. For some reason, it struck me that he might have been a submarine captain. Presently he began talking about poetry and told me he had written a volume that was privately printed. A few days later he brought in a copy. The verse was much in the vein of Benton's *This Is My Beloved*. He wondered if I would stock a dozen of them on a consignment basis. I agreed.

Why not? When he left, he said cryptically, "You're the only friend I have."

Months passed during which I heard nothing from him. Then one evening I saw a newspaper picture of my friend aboard a fine looking schooner tied up at the mouth of the Chicago River. He was sailing to the South Seas in it.

He came in a few days later to say goodbye. Of course I had failed to sell any of the poetry, so he suggested I keep the books until he returned from his voyage. As we shook hands, he was still tense and jumpy. A few months later he was dead, shot by a girl he had taken along. I had just recovered from reading the sensational press accounts of the tragedy when I received a phone call from the late poet's uncle, who said, "I know about your friendship with Jack and would appreciate it if you would give the reporters an interview as we absolutely refuse to do so ourselves." Before I knew it, I was being quoted in the papers about a man I had scarcely known and a book I couldn't sell. The girl in the case got some engagements as an exotic dancer after her release from a Cuban jail, but the affair did next to nothing for the book. Not even a murder scandal will sell poetry.

To everyone who brings me his writing, I protest that I am not an agent. But often it is hard to turn them away. There was the little gnarled old man with a few straggly long grey hairs for a beard who came in clutching a tired, worn briefcase. His story of persecution and cruel rejection was too much for me. "Let me see your book," I said. The soiled, yellow pages were brought out of the case, along with half a sandwich wrapped in Kleenex, and deposited gently on my desk. The manuscript was in longhand. It purported to tell the saga of man's continual search for personal freedom.

"How long have you been writing this book?" I said.

"All my life," he replied. He had once been a history professor he assured me.

"And what do you do now?"

A kind of cackle came out of him. "I am a presser of pants."

"And how did you come to bring this to me?"

"I watch you on television every morning."

"Well," I said, "I'm no publisher, but leave it with me. I'll try reading it over the weekend. When you come back for it, maybe I can tell you what to do next."

Or there was the woman who had written inspirational poetry since she was ten. She had paid to have one volume of verse printed, and now she had another. "This volume is for my mother," she said. "She is very sick. If I could get it published, I think it would help her. But I don't have the money to pay for it." And her voice trailed away into other worlds. She worked nights at a large office building. During the day, when she wasn't caring for her sick mother, she wrote poetry.

"May I see it, please?" And now I was stuck. "Leave it with me. I'll see what I can do." Of course I could do nothing. But how could I tell this fragile, helpless creature that even great poetry is unlikely to sell two thousand copies? I recalled Dr. Frieda Fromm-Reichmann once saying to me: "A good analyst must always have a rescue fantasy to offer." But I am not an analyst, rabbi, priest, or even a Miss Lonelyhearts.

A young man, hate and rebellion written terribly

across his face, accosted me unannounced and declared: "I've watched you on TV. You sound like a right guy. Here's my book. Find me a publisher. Everybody's a crook these days, but maybe you're not. Maybe you believe what you say. Well, here's your chance to prove it!" Then he rushed out, leaving the manuscript behind and me yelling after him, "Hey, wait a minute!" But he was gone.

It is not merely the poor and downtrodden or the hopeless nuts who seek fulfillment through publication. "If you can get my wife's book published, I'll give you ten thousand dollars," a wealthy customer told me. Another said, "Get this book published for me and I'll buy five thousand copies!" Another, who had certainly made his mark in business told me, "If I can get published, all my life will not have been lived in vain."

Touching and even terrifying as these thwarted impulses toward expression may be, virtually every example turns out to be deficient in two ways:

1. It is badly written.
2. Its philosophic content is borrowed instead of being distilled from the writer's own experience.

The second error is also a glaring defect in the work of many practicing and commercially successful novelists. For example: the writer who, in drawing a neurotic character, simply reproduces the appropriate behavior patterns as described in psychoanalytic literature. The result may be letter perfect as to accuracy and tailor-made to fit the requirements of the situation, but the final product is nothing but an empty shell.

In any event, a real writer is not just someone with a fierce urge or dominating fantasy about self-expression. He may well have a demon that drives him or he may find a way to knowledge out of the depths of personal frustration. But before all else, he is someone who has a feeling for the craft of handling the written word and the patience to try to discipline himself in this craft. The main thing to remember about a writer is that he makes it his business to put words together on a sheet of paper.

Beyond this, he may be any sort of person, of any physique, of any age, alcoholic or not, paranoid or not, cruel or not, drug addicted or not, horrible to women and children or not, teach Sunday School or not, anything you please. He can even engage in any vocation or profession, as long as he keeps going back to his desk and putting words together. He can be wealthy or have no money at all, and his personal life can be perfectly average and uneventful or utterly unbelievable. Just as long as he really works at words.

The level of his intention and his art may vary from writing for the newspapers to plumbing the depths of experience or pursuing some ultimate vision, but within the range he undertakes, the discipline of words calls also for the discipline of values, intelligence, emotion, perception. Writers who are serious about their business know these things, and the difficulties they present, too well to have to talk about them. In all my conversations with writers, I can recall few instances in which anybody ever talked directly about the art of writing.

In the case of professional writers, I have acted more often as a catalyst than as a volunteer agent. For example,

I abused as well as prodded Paul Molloy, the prize-winning columnist of the *Chicago Sun-Times,* until he turned his hand to a book. The simplicity and sincerity of his style has an undoubted appeal, as the success of the book, *And Then There Were Eight,* has proved. I am sure he would have written it anyway, ultimately, but even a fine talent can use encouragement.

I have also found it possible to help another type of writer — the expert in a special field who is perfectly qualified to write a type of book that is greatly needed. During the period when my psychiatric book speciality was at its peak, I became aware of the need for a single giant book on the whole story of psychiatry. Dr. Franz Alexander, then Director of the Chicago Institute for Psychoanalysis, was the obvious choice for such a monumental undertaking. No other great authority was so widely respected outside his particular field — not only among those in other "schools" of psychiatric thought, but among workers and scholars in every area concerned with the human psyche.

Dr. Alexander was the very first student at the Institute of Psychoanalysis founded by Freud in Vienna. I loved to listen to Dr. Alexander reminisce about his relationships with Freud and the original Seven and especially admired his view of the relationship of modern psychoanalysis to Spinoza's philosophy of the emotions. He was one of the few men I had encountered in this field who had a thorough background in philosophy. When I broached the idea of a monumental compendium, embracing the total field of psychiatry and psychoanalysis, historically and technically, he at first hesitated, then finally agreed — if the right publisher could be interested and if a fairly large advance could be obtained to help with the extensive research that would be involved.

Shortly thereafter, while on a trip to New York, I had lunch with Michael Bessie of Harper and Brothers and explained the idea to him. He was very much taken with it, and within a few weeks all of the details were worked out to Dr. Alexander's satisfaction. The work is still in progress, Dr. Alexander having retired to California to devote the greater part of his time to its completion.

Other books which I also managed to place for Chicago analysts were Irene Josslyn's *The Happy Child* and George Mohr's *Stormy Decade, Adolescence*.

But what of the young man or woman who has determined to devote himself to the difficult craft of writing, who has beaten out a book to his best ability, and is looking for a publisher? What do you do?

Well, of course, there is nothing to prevent you from bundling up your manuscript and mailing it to various publishers. Experience shows, however, that very few manuscripts submitted "cold" or, in the trade phrase, "over the transom" (obviously the mailman can't stick a manuscript through the letter slot), ever see the light of day. This doesn't mean that someone doesn't carefully consider the piece before attaching a rejection slip to it. I should say, however, that something of a very special literary quality — not the self-styled "advance guard" but the truly different, which has no audience ready-made and hence must create its own, the kind of literature which you just possibly might write (and which I think certainly is being written) and that could change the world through its extension of our resources of feeling and expression — does not stand too strong a chance of passing through the literate but patterned screening of publishers' manuscript readers. Furthermore, since each publishing house has a character all its own, the likelihood of any one manuscript ending up in the right place is a numbers game that can be quite disheartening to play.

Perhaps the best advice that can be given to the determined author is: Get a good agent. This is not necessarily easy and there are pitfalls, including sharks who prey upon the innocent for their own financial gain. A manuscript that comes into the publisher's office "cold" stands a better chance of receiving serious consideration than one sent under the auspices of a dubious agent. Nevertheless, a manuscript by an unknown writer usually gets a quicker reading if it comes through a recognized agent.*

With or without the help of an agent, the task is to try to place the book with some publisher. This task has become increasingly difficult unless the book is, by its very nature, a safe bet to sell. Nowadays the best bets are the so-called "non-books" — books specifically designed for selling, such as collections of humorous pictures and captions or volumes whose authors are not only well known in the entertainment world, but also carry a heavy clout with TV audiences: The Jack Paar Story, The Zsa Zsa Gabor Story, The Maurice Chevalier Story, The Harpo Marx

* An informative pamphlet on literary agents can be obtained from the Society of Authors Representatives, 522 Fifth Avenue, New York 10036.

Story—they may not all have exactly the same name and they may be written in greater or lesser part by relatively accomplished hacks, they may range from the fascinating to the disgusting in content, but they all exist for the same reason: there is a built-in audience that will buy them. Frankly, if Books and Brent had ever achieved network status, I could have done the same thing.

The problem is not that publishers will buy a sure thing. Of course they will and, within reason, why shouldn't they? The problem is that less and less is being published today that stands a chance of belonging in the realm of permanent literature. It is easier to get a book like this published, *about* books and writers (although not too popular a subject and therefore a fairly adventurous publishing undertaking), than it is to get the hard-wrought, significant works of some of the writers I have mentioned into print. Actually, most of the material that is selected for publication today is chosen precisely *because* it is temporary in value and appeal. Publishing, of course, is a difficult business and every book, in a sense, is a long shot, more likely to fail than to succeed in turning a profit. Most publishing houses have been built on the proposition that the successes must help subsidize the failures, but that this is the only way that the new and unknown talent, which will create the future of literature, can be developed. Publishing has never been like most manufacturing industries, where you can survey a new line before you try it, and drop it if it doesn't pay its way. In spite of all the tons of junk printed since Gutenberg, the glory and prestige of publishing is linked not with numbers of copies sold but numbers of enduring works produced. Virtually no one remembers the best sellers of 1900 or even 1950. But the great editors and publishers who nurtured, say, the talents of the 1920's have become part of literary history. A Maxwell Perkins couldn't exist in an industry that didn't care what it was doing or that wouldn't take its chances.

Taking a chance seems to be a custom that is going out of fashion — especially taking a chance on something you believe in. It is strange that this should be so, especially in business and industry, where the tax laws tend to encourage judicious failure ("product research," etc.) in any enterprise strong enough to be in the fifty-two percent bracket. Perhaps corporate structure is one of the factors that tend to close our horizons. A free individual can keep taking his chances until the world catches up with him. But the officer of a corporation who is responsible for justifying his actions to the board (and the board to the banks and the stockholders) does not have much leeway.

Both good books and bad books sell (and many books, both good and bad, fail to sell at all). A good book is, very simply, a revealing book. A bad book is bad because it is dull. Its author is obviously lying, not necessarily by purveying misinformation, but because he lards his work with any information that falls to hand — a sort of narrative treatment of the encyclopedia. A good book stirs your soul. You find yourself lost, not in an imaginary world (like the encyclopedia), but in a world where everything is understood. Readers and editors alike, no matter how debilitated, can detect this difference.

So, even, can the reviewers — largely a group of underpaid journalists and college professors who have a right, if any one does, to have become weary of letters. A writer friend of mine recently told of waiting at an airport for a plane that was late. He bought all three of the literary magazines obtainable from the newsstand and settled down to read. Every book review seemed to him written by someone who hated literature. He became utterly disgusted with both the reviews and the reviewers.

Considering the volume of publishing, how can it be so difficult to get good new books? There are not enough really significant titles coming out for me or anyone else to make a decent living selling them (I gave up trying with the Seven Stairs). When I talked with Mr. Simon, he assured me that Simon and Schuster and the book industry as a whole were booming with the mergers and the mushrooming educational market, but that the big problem was finding good writers and good books. I wonder if they are going about it properly. Somehow the prize contests and other subsidies never seem to bring genuine individual talent to the fore, and while everybody claims to be looking for something fresh, what gets bought looks suspiciously like the same old package.

Publishing has so often been (and in many cases, still is) a shoestring industry, that one gets a momentary lift from seeing it listed today on the board on Wall Street. But it is an open question whether the investors are supplying risk money for a cultural renaissance or buying into a sure thing: the increasing distribution of synthetic culture through textbooks and the propagation of standard classics and encyclopedias at cut-rate prices through the supermarkets.

Anyone who has given his heart and soul to literature and the arts is likely to regard everyone who pulls the financial strings in the communications world as a monster. But the commercial outlook on something like the retail book trade is so dispiriting that the wonder is anybody pays any attention to it whatever or publishes any books at all whose distribution depends upon such channels. In Chicago, for example, a center of about six million people, there are approximately five major bookstores (excluding religious and school book suppliers). Compared to this, I am told of a village in Finland of six thousand people where there are three bookstores doing a fine business! Now in my own shop I sell books, to be sure, but I also sell greeting cards, art objects manufactured by or for the Metropolitan Museum, paperbacks, records, and, at Christmas time, wrappings, ribbons, stickers, and miniature Santa Clauses. I still got into trouble one day when a woman came in and couldn't get a pack of pinochle cards. She thought I had a lot of nerve advertising books and not selling playing cards. Actually, "Bookstore" in America has come to mean a kind of minor supplier of paper goods and notions — and that is exactly what the great number of "Book Dealers — Retail" listed in the Chicago Redbook in fact are.

But you *can* buy a book in Chicago. Try it, however, in most of the cities across this vast country up to, say, 100,000 population. You'll be lucky to find a hardback copy of anything except the current best sellers. And in spite of the wonders of drug store paperbacks, a culture can't live and grow on reprints.

So let's face it. In a nation of 185 million people, some of whom are reasonably literate, a new book that sells ten to twenty thousand copies is regarded as pretty hot stuff. In an age of the mass market, this isn't hot enough to light a candle.

What to do about it? Well, in the first place, let's not be complacent about what's happening to American culture, to the American psyche. It isn't just the money-grubbing, the success-seeking; grubbing and striving, more or less, are a part of living. It is the emptiness, the meaninglessness. Nobody can get along without an interior life. The soul must be fed, or something ugly and anti-human fills the void. Spiritual nourishment is not a frill, apart from everyday necessity. The everyday and the ultimate expression of man do not exist apart. Synge remarked: "When men lose their poetic feeling for ordinary life and cannot write poetry of ordinary things, their exalted poetry is likely to lose its strength of exaltation, in the way men cease to build beautiful churches when they have lost happiness in building shops."

In the modern world, good reading offers one of the few means of getting back to one's self, of refreshing the spirit, of relating to the inward life of man. Through reading you can get acquainted all over again with yourself. You can stand being alone. You will look forward again to tomorrow.

Anything that stands in the way of this hope for renewal is an affront to man and a judgment on our times.

If the publishing industry has found a helpful new source of income through the present mania for education, fine. But a few extra years of education aren't going to change anybody's life. If we wait for a popular growth in "cultural maturity" to justify making more widely available the sustenance men need, it will come too late. There must be ways of cutting through the jungles of mass markets and mass media to reach, in a way that has not previously been possible, the much smaller but more significant audience of the consciously hungry. For as long as there are human souls still alive and sentient, there can be good books, good writers, even booksellers selling books again, paying their bills, earning a living.

Meantime, if you must be a writer, write seriously and well. Never pay for publication of your own book. Take your chances. If you succeed, fine. If not, then you must either persist in trying, time after time, or give up. Perhaps the present custodians of culture have their minds on other matters and do not wish to hear what you have to say. So be it. You will not be the first.

14

Books and Brent

WHEN I began to read, I fell in love with such a consuming passion that I became a threat to everyone who knew me. Whatever I was reading, I became: I was the character, Hamlet or Lear; I was the author, Shelley or Stendhal. When I was seized by sudden quirks, jerks, and strange gestures, it was not because I was a nervous child — I was being some character.

One morning when I awoke, I looked into the mirror and discovered that one part of my head seemed bigger than the other. I ate my breakfast in silence with my three sisters gathered about the table watching me. When I suddenly looked up, I thought I saw them exchanging meaningful glances.

"Do you see something strange about me?" I asked.

They shook their heads and suppressed a giggle.

My mother, washing dishes at the sink, stopped and looked at me, too.

"Do you see anything unusual about me?" I said. She didn't.

I got up and, standing in the middle of the floor, bent my head to one side and said, "Look, my head is swelling!"

My sisters laughed wildly, while my mother cried, "What are we going to do with this silly boy? What are we going to do?"

My knowledge, they assured me, was coming out of my head. And I told them this was not funny at all.

When I went back to the mirror, I liked my face much better. The forehead was showing some wrinkles. Lines were appearing at the mouth. The eyes seemed more in keeping with what might be expected of a thinker or poet. Before I had begun to read, this face certainly had appeared more ordinary — just smooth and clean and nothing else. Now that I had begun to peer a little into the minds of great men, something was entering my soul that reflected itself in my face. I was sure of it. Naturally, the idea that filling my head with knowledge might cause it to burst was nonsense, but I certainly was cramming in an oddly miscellaneous assortment of facts, dates, events, phrases, words, snatches of everything. I never read systematically. I read everything, and I think still that it is simply stupid to tell boys and girls to read certain books between the ages of nine and twelve, other books between sixteen and twenty, etc. I got lost in the paradise of books and it wrecked me forever — destroyed any possibility of my becoming a "successful" man, saved me from becoming a killer in the jungle of material ambition.

I think prescribed reading is the enemy of learning, and today it is probably the end of culture. As a boy, I devoured all the Sax Rohmer mysteries, the Rover Boys, the Edgar Rice Burroughs *Men of Mars* and the Tarzan series; I read *Penrod and Sam, Huckleberry Finn, Tom Sawyer* — all with equal enthusiasm. This is where it begins. Taste can come later.

There is a certain point, once enthusiasm is engendered, when a good teacher can open doors for you. I had such a teacher, and later a friend, in Jesse Feldman. His enthusiasm supported my own, and at the same time he held the key to the wealth of possibilities that literature offers. He was a scholar, but his real scholarship resided in his love for people. He believed ideas could change human hearts. He inspired me by making me wonder about everything. He showed me that the worst sin of which I might be capable would be to become indifferent to the human spirit.

It was Jesse who introduced me to Jack London's *Martin Eden.* I was seventeen. Then *Les Misérables, Nana,* and *Anna Karenina* set me off like a forest fire. There was no stopping me. I had to read everything. I plunged into Hardy's *Return of the Native* with pencil in hand, underlining and writing my thoughts in the margins. I loved to argue with the author and the need to make notations made it terribly important to own my own books, no matter how long it took to save the money to buy them. It was fun to look at books, to touch them, to think of the next purchase.

I read Dickens until I couldn't see straight. I read Goethe's *Faust* and thought secretly that the author was a pompous ass. Years later I again read it and became fascinated with the entire Faustian legend. This is the way it should be. You don't have to get it the first time.

I can remember when I first read *The Brothers Karamazov* and how it unnerved me. The book created such fierce anxieties within me that I couldn't finish it. I had to wait a number of years before I could tolerate the strain it put on my nervous system.

Later Jesse gave me my first introduction to Thomas Mann and Jules Romain. I read Henry Hudson's *Green Mansions* and to this day I can't forget Abel and Rima. I read Dreiser's *Sister Carrie* and loved his social criticism, his amazing bitterness, his terrible writing. I memorized the *Ode to the West Wind* and began my Shelley imitations, adopting, among other things, his habit of reading standing up. I read Galsworthy and wrote long précis of his wonderful short stories. My reading was for myself, my notebooks were for myself, my thoughts and ideas were for myself.

Although I was seldom without a book at any time, the very best time to read was on Saturday mornings. Normally my mother baked on Friday and she had a genius for failing to remember that something was in the oven. So if I was lucky, there would be plenty of cookies or cake or strudel left, slightly burned, that nobody else would touch. I loved it. Then, too, the house was strangely still on Saturday mornings. No one was home and I could turn up the volume on the phonograph as loudly as I wished and sit and listen and read and eat cake. It was marvelous.

Sometimes a single vivid line was the reward for days

of desultory reading. I remember first coming across Carlyle's remark in *Heroes and Hero-Worship,* "The Age of Miracles is forever here!" and how I plucked that phrase and kept repeating it even in my darkest moments. Again, after finishing *Moby Dick,* a book I took straight to my heart, I began a research job on Melville and encountered a letter written to Hawthorne that marked me for life. I was reading at the public library, and as closing time approached I began to race madly through the books I had gathered, trying to find something that would tell me what Melville was like. Suddenly my heart skipped a beat and I knew that I had found it (child of innocence that I was, bent on researching the whole world, ancient and modern): "My development," Melville wrote, "has been all within a few years past. Until I was twenty-five, I had no development at all. From my twenty-fifth year I date my life. Three weeks have scarcely passed, at any time between then and now, that I have not unfolded within myself."

Closing time was called and I went out into the solitary night, walking thoughtfully home, thinking, thinking, thinking. I didn't want money or success or recognition. I didn't want a single thing from anybody. I wanted only to be alone, to read, to think . . . to unfold.

One year I'd be interested in literature, the next in philosophy, the following in physics or chemistry or even neurology. Everything interested me. Who cared what I ate or how I dressed? I cared only for the words between covers. I was safe so long as I didn't fall in love . . . this I knew from Schopenhauer. Spengler fascinated me. *The Decline of the West* was so brilliantly written, it had a scheme . . . and it was such a fraud. But I was learning how to read and how to think through what I was reading. I disliked Nietzsche and only later came to see him as one who was saying in very bald terms: Don't sell out! Stop wasting your time predicting the future of mankind, but become an active part in creating it.

I had long known the Old Testament, but now I became attracted to the New Testament and the figure of Jesus. I memorized the Sermon on the Mount and spent sleepless nights arguing with myself. I went wild over Tawney's *The Acquisitive Society* and Max Weber's *The Protestant Ethic* had a tremendous effect on me and sent me back to reading Washington, Jefferson, Hamilton, and Benjamin Franklin. I was beginning to suspect that I was too deeply influenced by European literature and not enough by American. Why was I drawn to Kafka and Mann and Gide and Proust and Anatole France and Huysmans and not to Howells and Emerson and Whitman and Hawthorne and Melville and Thoreau? I set myself a course of study and luckily started with Hawthorne. Had I started with Howells, I have a strong notion I'd have given up. But I liked Hawthorne, and this led to Melville and here I found my God and my America. His involuted writing was perfect for me and this in turn led to Henry James. When James made the remark about the gorgeous wastefulness of living, I knew he was right. In the eyes of the world I lived in, I was wasting my time. Many of my friends by now had good jobs selling insurance or automobiles or were on the way to becoming successful junior executives. And I? Well, I was reading! I always worked, to be sure, but at odd jobs only. If I went to school during the day, then I worked at night. If I attended night school, then I worked during the day. But what the job was made no difference to me.

Sometimes I did pause to ask myself where this was going to lead. There was the day I was being interviewed for a job at Woolworth's and the man asked, "What do you know?" I started to tell him what I knew about the various schools of literature and philosophy and he stopped me cold, saying, "You know too much about the wrong things. We can't hire you." This knocked me out for days.

What did I want to be? Did I have to become something? Did I have to have some kind of social approval? For a time I went around in a state of near collapse. First I decided upon medicine as a good practical profession with a lot of good basic knowledge behind it. Then I felt that perhaps I should be a lawyer. I was generally regarded as a good speaker and I had an idea that criminal lawyers were exciting people. Then I thought possibly I ought to be an architect. But nothing fitted. Finally I decided. I was going to teach.

To my shocked amazement, I discovered that all my years spent at college, all my study, the range of knowledge I had sought to embrace, meant absolutely nothing in the eyes of the master educators. I was deficient in what were called Education Courses. There was nothing for me to do but to take them.

In all my life in the classroom, I had never encountered such a waste of time, such stupidity, such a moral outrage! The courses were insipid and the teachers themselves knew nothing whatever. It was either insane nonsense or an organized racket from top to bottom: courses on the theory of education (I had already gotten my theory from Samuel Butler and George Meredith, neither of whom the educators seemed to have heard of), courses on educational psychology (something completely occult), courses on techniques, courses on I.Q. measurements, courses on the art of choosing a textbook. By the time I had finished my required work in education, I could not have been less inspired to be a teacher. I had heard a great deal about the smug middle class and their valueless world, and have since encountered them and it, but I shall be happy to exhibit any group of typical specimens of this order as examples of vibrant living and exciting intellect compared to a meeting of "educators." No wonder books are dying!

In those depression days, it seemed to me that the education world was something invented to keep some walking zombies busy. But it turned out that the educators got in on the ground floor of a good thing. With the present hue and cry for education and more education, their job is cut out for them: tests and more tests, techniques and more techniques.

We don't need more educators; we need more *teachers*. And especially teachers of literature. Not teachers who are smug in their learning and want to impose value judgments on others. But teachers who are alive with love and enthusiasm, whose own experience with art and letters has made them a little less ashamed to be members of the human race. Not teachers armed with a book list, but with a personal addiction to reading as a never ending source of generous delight. Not experts in testing and guidance, but people with enough faith in youth to inspire them to find their own way and make their own choices, to taste the exhilaration of stumbling and bumbling on their own amid all the wonders and ups and downs of the human quest for understanding. We need teachers who will stimulate, provoke, and challenge, instead of providing crutches, short cuts, and easy directions. There is just no point in building all those new school buildings unless we have more Jesse Feldmans to fill them with the realization that the aim of education is to help man become human.

I seldom go back to where the Seven Stairs used to be. It is hard to visualize it as it once was. The old brownstone has a new face, the front bricked up and the door bolted. Business is good on the Avenue, but many of the people who come in seem tight-lipped and hurried. The Seven Stairs is not there either.

But when we start looking up old places, it means we have forgotten them as symbols. The Seven Stairs was an adventure of the heart . . . a personal search for the Holy Grail, a quest that still continues. Each step up the stairs has brought crisis and someone to help me overcome that crisis and move on to the next. And seven being an enchanted number and stairs moving inward and out-

ward as well as upward and downward, the ascent is un-
ending, and every step a new beginning, where we must
stand our ground and pay the price for it.

There is a Seven Stairs lurking unbeknown down every
street as there was for me on a summer day, getting off
the bus at the wrong corner on my way to meet my
brother-in-law for lunch and walking along Rush Street,
fascinated with the strangeness of the neighborhood. I
was reading all the signs, for no purpose at all, but one
that said, "Studio for Rent," stuck with me. I turned back
to look at it again before rounding the corner to go to my
appointment.

I met Mel in the kind of restaurant that is exactly the
same everywhere, the same I had been in a few weeks earlier while awaiting my army discharge in San Francisco,
the same fixtures, the same food, the same waitresses, the
same voices. But as I leaned across the table and began
talking, I experienced a sudden excitement and an idea
generated which I announced with as much assurance as
though it had been the outcome of months of deliberation.
Fifteen years later, I can still see Mel's jaw drop and his
momentary difficulty in breathing when I told him I had
decided I wanted to go into business.

"What kind of business?" he said, finally.

I told him that what Chicago needed was a real bookstore. It seemed to me that I had always had visions of
my name across a storefront: Stuart Brent, Bookseller. I
made him go with me to look at the "for rent" sign, then
together we went to see the landlord — my terrible, mincing, Machiavellian, fat little landlord.

We borrowed the keys and went back to see the studio. Mel didn't really want to go along, but somehow I had to have him with me. If the quarters turned out to be disappointing, I didn't think I could stand it. But when we opened the door, the hot, dirty room was magic. As I looked up at the sixteen foot ceiling, I imagined pretty Victorian society girls dressing here for the ball. I wasn't seeing the room. I had just stepped through the door from Berkeley Square.

"Isn't this rather small for what you have in mind?" Mel said.

"No, no," I said, "it's just fine. Everything is just fine!"

Postscript—1973

Francis Bacon long ago spoke of the human understanding as an irregular mirror which distorts and discolors the light of nature: "Numberless are the ways in which the affections color and infect the understanding."

Through this imperfect glass the decade since *The Seven Stairs* was originally published seems strange, indeed, while the vanished world the book reflected often seems rather more real and immediate, and certainly more comprehensible, than that of the years which have followed.

Ten years ago, I did not find society in general or the publishing world in particular offering much hospitality to manifestations of the human spirit. Since then, things have deteriorated. On the one hand there is the possibly fatal corrosion of an immoral war. You would think no one in government had read enough history to know how easily an army can be defeated when the society for which it presumably is fighting walks away from it: Russia 1917; Germany 1918; Italy 1944; next? On the other hand, there is the unremitting din of every manner of crisis. I must say that, in their book buying habits, an impressive number of people appear to recognize that something is wrong with themselves and with society. We sell books such as the popular transactional psychiatric volume, *I'm O. K.— You're O. K.*, by the hundreds. We sell books that tell you what steps to take to safeguard the environment, how to counter the pollution of the air, the contamination of the water supply, the killing off of wildlife, and the rising noise levels of cities. From the themes of the books appearing in greatest profusion today—racial tension, youth revolution, urban crisis, military takeover, population, cancer—you would think an aroused populace were about to root out error wherever found, supported by a publishing industry alert to its social responsibilities.

This is not the case.

The overwhelming number of books published since the mid-1960's concerning Blacks, Puerto Ricans, American Indians, Mexican Americans, heads, doves, welfare mothers, migrant workers, homosexuals, and other minorities spring less from a heightened social conscience among publishers than from a fixation upon headlines. And the headlines do not necessarily sell books. Further, it is impossible to write and publish a profound book within the time span of a breaking news story.

What's actually selling today is books on necromancy and general otherworldliness. Nothing has amazed me more than the unearthing of Hermann Hesse's novels and the sudden enthusiasm for them. The young have bought *Siddartha* by the thousands, the *Tibetan Book of the Dead*

(admired in the '30's by Ezra Pound) has sold by the carload, and writers like Watts and others introducing Zen
and Karma have enjoyed a vogue previously reserved for
popular charlatans.

What disturbs me more than these vagaries has been the
decline of the novel from a finely tuned instrument of the
imagination to a sick exhibition of sexual violence addressed
to men and women who no longer feel.

In spite of all the self-help books, as well as the more
serious treatment of man's problems and potentials, no one
can offer such valid guidance as the novelist. No one else
permits you to enter imaginatively into his world in quite
the same way. Proust thought this to be the prime function
of imaginative literature: to release the reader from the
bondage of living out his life within the limitations of a
single consciousness.

If we lose the powerful and liberating force of imaginative literature, the depersonalization of modern life will just
about be complete. The enjoyment of the printed page has
two unique characteristics, both highly personal: it is a
private event and it *demands* participation. You can be
sitting in a room with a hundred people, but the minute
you begin to read, you are alone. Furthermore, even if the
content of what you are reading is relatively superficial, the
experience of reading is never passive. *Nothing* happens on
the printed page. It happens in your head. *You* are an engaged participant. Literature alone among the arts can
never be merely a spectator sport.

Chicago already has what it takes in the way of great art,
great music, and great buildings to establish its credentials

as a cultural capital. It is making headway in contemporary art and experimental theatre. In the amenities that support a cosmopolitan culture, including fine shops, good food, and good accommodations, Chicago easily can hold its own and, unlike New York City, it has not given up graciousness.

But literature remains peripheral to our community life. The European café, of course, as a place for literary conversation, is something that just does not exist in our culture or our economy. But neither does the bookstore. It didn't in 1945 when I started The Seven Stairs, as my Father would have said, out of *votta* and *schmatta* (cotton and rags). It assuredly doesn't today.

Nonetheless, in 1968, when the opportunity arose to obtain extra space, doubling the size of my Michigan Avenue shop, I felt something stir in my psyche. It wasn't long before I was off to Manhattan, where I spent days watching book store operations and searching for something equivalent to Blackwell's in Oxford, which rightly or not had always symbolized for me the ideal of a bookshop. I found numerous stores offering books, but no one with whom I could *talk* about books until I reached the Gotham Book Mart and engaged in conversation with its famous 77-year-old proprietress, Miss Frances Steloff. It was not merely the nostalagic interest of her firsthand reminiscences of Joyce, Eliot, and Pound. It was an encounter with one of the passionate believers in the written word. She gave you the desire to become involved. You were no longer an outsider looking in.

Well, there it was, a true bookstore, and I was grateful

for it and for the link it provided me with the literary ferment of the '20's and the '30's. Could this be done for the living present and could it be done here in Chicago?

Twenty-five years before, when I opened on Rush Street, I wasn't really thinking about Chicago as a literary community and I didn't even know any authors. I just had a personal, romantic dream about being a bookseller, and the temerity to try to do it by myself and for myself. As reported in these pages, the dream came true and for five years The Seven Stairs flourished as a place where people could and did come to share in an atmosphere where literature was respected. When I moved the shop to Michigan Avenue, I'd hoped everything would carry over. In addition to the street-level floor, the new store had a fine air-conditioned basement room, which I fitted out as a meeting place. But it didn't work out that way. I was still running a one-man operation and I couldn't be downstairs talking with friends and upstairs selling books at the same time. Gradually the regulars who had gathered around the apple barrel at The Seven Stairs drifted away.

Nevertheless, the new location made possible the increasing volume of business that I needed to support a growing family and keep my accountant out of psychoanalysis. And the joy of the thing remained, the delight of selling good books and talking about them.

Why not be content, then, in one's middle years and forget the vacant store-space next door? Let someone else break his heart. I'm on the floor twelve hours a day as it is.

But there was nothing for it. A crazy enthusiasm stirred

my imagination and in a very short time I had persuaded Norman de Hahn, an old classmate and superb architect, to draw up the plans for a new addition to the bookstore.

He was willing to listen to my wild outbursts about what a real bookshop should be and to translate them into design ideas that combined tradition and dignity with a modern panache, including even a circular staircase. It was no automated supermart, but a haven for browsing, filled with nooks and surprises, radiating about an island of oak cabinets and shelves.

Cost estimates were drawn up. Financing was secured—not a $300 loan such as that which launched The Seven Stairs, but $50,000: more than I had ever owed in my life!

If the bank had that kind of faith in me, I certainly should have courage to go ahead. So ahead we did, with Norman Cohen of Inland Construction commanding the crew that broke through the walls, ripped out the ceilings, applied new plaster, built and glazed a new front, and eventually installed the new furnishings and equipment, every detail of which had been worked out with loving care. Every detail, that is, except for a host of crude practicalities that Norman de Hahn and I had been too carried away even to contemplate.

For a time, all went well. I never closed the shop a day, even when they were drilling through the concrete floor to make room for that circular staircase. Business was conducted as usual. But one morning, Norman Cohen called a meeting. He and his chief supervisor, Mr. Blake, and Norman de Hahn and I sat down and carefully went over the items on a sheet of paper and agreed that were all correct and added them up. The grand total was $97,000.

I tried to control my emotions and felt the growing dampness around my collar. Then I was gripped by the same feeling that came over me when I first wanted to buy that acre of land at Bark Point. I wanted it, and nothing was going to interfere with satisfying that want, least of all money. Presently I was able to look up from the sheet of figures. Everyone was trying to smile and saying things like, "Stuart, we'll give you time," or "Don't worry about this. We trust you."

"Thanks," I said. "Go ahead. I'll get the money."

We shook hands all around and I started to walk out. Norman de Hahn followed me. "I'm sorry," he said. "Don't worry about my fee until you can afford it." I felt warmed by his genuine dismay.

As I started out for the bank, I recalled the walk I had taken along Michigan Avenue years before, when I was turned down for a loan of $5,000. Now I needed a *second* $50,000. What should I tell the banker? What excuse or rationalization could I offer? Better to blurt out the truth. Then what? If refused an additional loan, I would sell my house and move the family somewhere—perhaps into the store basement. That new store must be built!

I heard myself having trouble enunciating, as my banker, Stanley Walton, listened. The words seemed to be slithering here and there, but the meaning was very clear. I finished with a lumpy throat, sweaty hands, and the determination that if he said no and demanded return of the $50,000 already advanced, I would just go home, call the real estate broker, and tell Hope to start packing.

Then I heard him saying through a thin smile, and as though from a rather considerable distance, "We've gone along with you for fifty, we might as well go along for another fifty. Just keep that door open to the customers. You'll make it just fine."

I left the bank with the feeling that I had to do something for someone more or less immediately or burst. So I went to Saks Fifth Avenue and bought Hope a dress.

While writing the Bark Point chapter of this book, I was reminded of the occasion when we nearly lost our beloved golden retriever, Mr. Toast, on the way to the Point. We had all gotten out of the station wagon at a gas station, then piled back in the car without him. We didn't miss him until hours after we reached Bark Point. The odd thing was that most of the children though they remembered Toast getting out of the car when we arrived at the cottage. With help from Robert Parrish, who has assisted me over the years in literary enterprises, I elaborated this anecdote into a story which my children found appealing. After *The Seven Stairs* was published, I submitted the Toast story to my editor. Before long, the word came back from the experts that the manuscript was unsuitable for publication because it was too long for younger readers and too short for older readers.

Sympathizing with the frustrated authors who have so often asked my help in finding a publisher, I tried Viking Press, which has a distinguished list of children's books.

They accepted *The Strange Disappearance of Mr. Toast* on its own terms and published it in 1964. It was favorably received and a sequel was written. Working with Annis Duff, my editor at Viking, was a fine experience and I developed great respect for her judgment and for the role that the vanishing breed of great editors has played in literary production. When she left Viking because of ill health, I left also, finding a sympathetic aid to my endeavors in Lippincott, which published the third Toast book in the spring of 1971. Shortly before its publication date, Toast died at the age of 13.

There will be other dogs in the Brent household, but we will not know them in quite the same way, for we cannot share with them the experiences of the decade that we shared with Toast. His affectionate responsiveness was part of our being, and at the same time his individuality extended our capability for kinship with all living things.

His favorite spot was in front of the fireplace, and in the last few months before he died, he was there more often than not. He looked well. Oh, his muzzle was turning grey and he was lame in one leg and he had a little trouble getting in and out of the station wagon. Also, he was quite deaf.

But until nearly the end, he was strong and active and practiced the art of the retriever with unfailing perfection. No ball was tossed into the air or stick thrown down the ravine that was not promptly recovered and returned by Mr. Toast.

David, the oldest of our eight children, used to become greatly annoyed when people spoke of Toast as "almost human." They meant well. But the wonderful thing about

Toast was that he was a superb *animal.* He wasn't an imitation, "almost" man. He was a dog and gave what only a dog could offer.

Hope and I bought him on a cold January night in 1956. We had a flat tire en route and I lost the way several times. Still, we persisted and ultimately found the home in Northbrook that housed the future protector of the Brent family.

We were ushered down into the basement, part of which was fenced off with wire mesh. The lady of the house opened a kind of make-do door and out came tumbling eight fat golden retrieiver puppies, bouncing and falling over each other. They ran across our feet, rolled behind us, leaped around us, and generally cavorted for perhaps fifteen minutes. One puppy kept pawing at my feet until I picked him up, when he promptly kissed me. I passed him to Hope and he kissed her, too. We had been selected.

Settling on an appropriate name was more difficult. We studied the puppy carefully. His coat was reddish brown, his ears were long and curly, his eyes deep brown. He had a short tail and *very* large paws. Whatever he was named, Mister should be the prefix, we decided, because he was so important looking. And since he was the color of toast, why not call him Mr. Toast?

He was just eight weeks old that winter night when we brought him home. While reading advertisements for dogs, Hope had asked, "Is a golden retriever a *little* dog?"

"Certainly," I said. "Perfect for an apartment."

Until he was eight months old, his favorite hiding place was beneath our bed. As he became larger, it was an increasing scramble to get under the bed and a virtual impossibility to get out. Finally, he would lift himself up, forcing the mattress to rise, with Hope and me on it!

His increasing stature caused no end of trouble. When he entered the living room, his joyfully wagging tail would sweep the dishes off the coffee table. After suffering innumerable scoldings, he learned to arrest his bounding approach with a frantic skid, at the same time keeping his tail between his legs, a posture both ridiculous and touching.

He was a fine companion; loving, faithful, highly responsible. And he was mysterious. Beneath the manner of the civilized dog lay other patterns of intelligence and memory. Often while playing on a beach, he would retrieve a sizeable rock, one weighing perhaps two pounds. He would move it carefully to a spot where the sand was soft, then look to see if anyone was watching. If someone was, he spread his front feet around the rock and waited for the intruders to go away or mind their own business.

Then when no one was paying attention, he would begin to dig, moving first one powerful front paw, then the other, digging on either side of the rock. This would go on rhythmically for perhaps ten minutes. Suddenly he would stop and let out a low, menacing growl. The growl rose in pitch, then a roar filled the air and he began digging again, sand flying out of the hole and landing behind him. The rock lay at the bottom of a three-foot pit, and Toast could barely continue the operation without falling in. Still he raged at the rock and dug until exhausted by an obsession as strange to us as so many of our motives must have been to him.

Toast in his youth was powerful and active, in his middle years he fathered many magnificent retrievers, and in his declining years he took things easier, slept more, and watched our children grow.

Then there was the day when Joshua, our four year old, tossed a stick down the ravine for Toast to fetch, and Toast couldn't make it up the bank. Hope and Amy had to rescue him. Our old dog was dying.

He slept a great deal by the fire. When I bent down and touched him, he awoke, saw who I was, and nestled his big head in my lap, looking up at me.

"My puppet is sad," Joshua told his nursery school teacher the day after Toast departed.

"Why?" she asked.

"Just sad," he said. "Very sad."

In addition to marrying me against all odds, mothering our eight children, and maintaining a special self that is for me, Hope has brought her experience as a teacher and her sensitivity to bear upon the creation of a wonderful children's book department in our store. At this particular juncture, introducing the young to the sustaining delights of literature is a mission of the greatest urgency. And at the same time that imaginative writing for the adult has declined to a sad level, books for children seem to me to be steadily gaining in vitality and general merit. Perhaps writing for children is the best field for the serious and sensitive creative writer. Certainly a literary generation that produces a few classics for children will not be a total loss.

Whenever possible, I answer the phone at the shop my-self. One morning the caller was the wife of an elderly author whose works, for reasons both literary and senti-mental, have been very close to my heart. She told me that the publisher had not even advertised her husband's most recent novel—a charming minor work—that it had re-ceived scarcely any reviews, and that I appeared to be the only bookseller in America who was prompting it. No one at the publishing house would even talk with her, she said, and her husband was ill and upset.

I was shocked. It did not suprise me that the book might not have a large sale. But this should not have mattered. This was a man who for half a century had always written well and who over those years had had large successes, producing substantial revenue for his publishers. But this publishing house had become part of a corporate con-glomerate. Its management was responsible to the stock-holders, whose ideals and interests are judged, apparently, to be neither literary nor humane. Few American pub-lishers are left who are accountable to themselves. The subsidizing of volumes whose distinction is not reflected in large sales is simply out of the question. The basis for justifying editorial selection has become increasingly crass.

A number of great houses, respected for generations of service to American letters, exist in name only, and even then, sometimes in peculiarly hyphenated form, as ap-pendages to the synthetic field of school textbook produc-tion.

Just as the publisher-author-relationship has tended to evaporate, so has the relationship between publisher and bookseller. To say that the heart and spirit have gone out of the publishing business sounds unduly romantic. Anyone who has made money out of publishing in the past 50 years has had to have more going for him than art for art's sake. He's had to be a pretty hard-headed character. But he was not just a businessman, just someone in a line to make money. The important publishers actually related to the field—to book writing, bookmaking, bookselling.

In my early days in the book business, it was often as not the president or the sales manager of the publishing house who answered the phone when I called, asking for another extension in meeting my financial obligations. The usual response was, in effect: "Look, kid, we need you to sell Kafka."

The heartwarming thing about this to the young, under-capitalized bookseller was not only that people in the industry cared about him; it was also that they knew Kafka!

As I have recounted, most of the heads of the great publishing houses took time to visit my shop when they were in Chicago. Their economic motivation was often intense, but so was their interest in the business they were in.

Today little enthusiasm and joy are detectable in the publishing offices, where payments are due in 30 days and the sales managers tell you they treat everyone the same. But everyone is *not* the same. The small independent book dealers cannot compete on the same footing with the wholesalers, the book clubs, and the chain stores.

When I started selling books, payment of accounts in anything under 120 days assured a perfect credit rating, and a real bookseller never thought of returning an unsold book in less than 18 months. Selling a book was and is a minor miracle, impossible of accomplishment without wild enthusiasm. This miracle can only occur when one is imbued with the feeling of earning his living while being compensated by something else.

But little purpose is served by protesting that today's credit managers function like Gestapo agents or that the heart has gone out of the business: there is really no one to complain to, no one to answer the letter, nobody there.

The exceptions are significant, greatly to be treasured, and small in number. The names of five important houses come quickly to mind, all of which remain under individual ownership, continue to publish real books, and take an interest in what they are doing.

Obviously this is something to hold onto, but it is scarcely enough, in a country of nearly 200 million souls, to perpetuate either bookmaking or bookselling as activities of consequence. This is not merely a matter of the obsolescence of a certain kind of merchandising. The impending catastrophe lies in the cutting off of effective channels for an irreplaceable mode of human expression.

Today I have the bookshop of my dreams. It is a memorial. I work the same long hours as before and keep rehearsing the same dreams. Dreams, like love, become a habit. And habit, as a life force, is not to be despised. Without it there is no explanation of life and work: both are biological and spiritual acts of faith.

Fifteen years ago, when I started to think about writing *The Seven Stairs*, the late Bennett Cerf advised me not to do so. I had not lived long enough to write a memoir, he told me.

Bennett may have been right, but for the wrong reasons.

Only the young have the capacity to celebrate their every action as the most amazing happening since the Creation, their every perception and emotion as a fresh conquest in the struggle for awareness. The name of each person who befriended—or who offended—one's emerging self blazes with significance. The worthwhile memorials commemorate our youth. We fight briefly to become; the rest is memory and, at times, literature.

The Seven Stairs never presumed to capture the essence of an age or to document much of anything except some remembered footsteps, foolishness, heartbreaks, and epiphanies. Yet, from these personal notations, some characteristics of the scene may emerge, the country we inhabited, the half-forgotten faces.

Where are they now? This is the easy and inviting game to play with an account strewn with its share of names and citations for achievement or potential. A few should be footnoted. Studs Terkel, then undervalued, has gained national recognition as the modern Mayhew (whereas I was plugging for him as the most creative of TV personalities.) Nelson Algren, by all accounts, remains Nelson Algren. Before the children of affluence took to the street in large numbers and before dope became a vital ingredient of "the scene," Nelson wrote about the "wild side" with a clear understanding of what it meant to be a loser. His former compatriot, Jack Conroy, may or may not still be a popular favorite with readers in the USSR, but it is known

that he has retired from the drudgery of work on encyclopedias and is engaged in writing his autobiography. Few
men know more about the 1930's era, its people, and its
artistic movements. And in a field marked by shifting al-
legiances, no man has been a better friend to his fellow
writers.

This book also tells of my encounters with television
and summer theatre. Of those with whom I worked in
Chicago television, only Marty Faye remains a regular
purveyor of talk and entertainment. Tom Duggan, who
became a TV personality through his capacity for getting
into trouble, is dead. My seven years of book talks termi-
nated shortly after "Red" Quinlan lost his battle to create
an alternative kind of commercial TV. My experience in
the theatre was much more ephemeral, and those with
whom my brief acquaintance in this arena took place are
departed, also. The talented Karen Kupcinet was the victim of a senseless crime and the gracious Linda Darnell
died in a fire.

Things change. Besides books and records, I today sell
greeting cards and Creative Playthings (toys that involve
you or your children in activities conducive to wonder and
self-awareness).

But for playing cards, you'll have to go next door to
Woolworth's. I have lost some friends and customers and
gained others about whom I should like to write at length
some day, such as Marvin Glass, a genius in his field of
creating toys and an informed and sustaining influence in
most areas of the human spirit, or the indomitable Bert
Liss, a South Bend, Indiana, businessman who doesn't

know how to capitulate. Or the manufacturer, Dave Borowitz, an addicted bibliophile, whose steps I should like to follow through the bookshops of London; or James Simmons, whose love of fine books is both sensual and dedicated; or Arthur Edelstein, a merchant whom I have known for 25 years and whose selfless giving arouses awe as well as deep affection.

In revisiting the days of the Seven Stairs, I see some figures in much different focus, for example, Dr. Lionel Blitzten's analysand, Dr. J. Dennis Freund and his wife Jerry, whose manifold kindnesses to me were too great for me to acknowledge then. The future may already be determined for us, but we continually remake the past.

Postscript—1988

I HAVE always felt that my relationship with my customers is both personal and mutual. When my wife, Hope, died in 1984, I found that this was, indeed, the case. Outside my own family, there proved to be no greater source of strength than the kind and supportive words of customers who had been touched by Hope's vital spirit.

For a period of time after Hope's death, it appeared that an economically feasible lease for a shop like ours on Michigan Avenue had become out of the question. The issue of whether Stuart Brent Books would endure attracted national media attention. As it turned out, this tempest in a teapot was related to my landlord's negotiations to sell the property, a shockingly valuable piece of land. The purchaser proved to be Ambassador Daniel Terra, who acquired the property in connection with his remarkable Museum of American Art project. Ambassador Terra offered Stuart Brent Books a reprieve, and as of this date we are still doing business on the Avenue.

The clouds which so darkened those recent years have finally been put to magical flight by my marriage to Carolyn Wilkinson, a medical scientist who has taught me to live in the timeless present. Obviously a guardian angel watches over me.

How much there still is to do in this age of apparent lunacy! When the fortieth anniversary of my business was being celebrated last year, the Chicago author and educator Richard Stern, who, like Saul Bellow, writes in a voice that is unmistakably his own, sent me this note:

"I wanted to come to your fortieth-anniversary party. You've not only been the synagogue of books, you've been my personal rabbi. (I don't have, never had my own synagogue.) I owe you for your cheer, your beautiful energy, and above all, your belief in me.

"Instead of going to your celebration, I descended into the hell of my students' papers. Stuart, the Dark Ages aren't coming, they're here. These bright, affectionate, enthusiastic young men and women are unable to write five pages of coherent prose. Their confusion, their carelessness, their illogic constitute a mental AIDS. They ripped me apart . . . So there it is, you down there, I here and between us . . . the sewer."

Aside from this, Carolyn and I are planting strawberries and raspberries when we go to the farm, fishing for steelheads in Lake Superior, trying to indulge the children and, so far as possible, avoiding fools.

One Hundred
Best Books

LISTS OF 100 this or that exert curious fascination. Recently I have been running up my personal list of 100 "best books"—not necessarily the books that critics say are masterpieces or teachers require you to read or *The New York Times* recommends, but books that have had special meaning for me. The importance of a book lies in the process it initiates in the reader. As Proust said: "Reading is at the threshold of spiritual life; it can introduce us to it; it does not constitute it."

Often the circumstances under which we read have an important part in the process. With this in mind, I have not only chosen my 100 best books, but also suggested the places or conditions that may be most favorable for reading them. Otherwise I shall make no comment on my selections; if you enjoy them, you will have your own reasons.

In any case, here we go with Brent's 100 favorites.

Reading While Eating Alone

1. Him with His Foot in His Mouth   *Saul Bellow*
2. Portrait of Jennie   *Robert Nathan*
3. A Handful of Dust   *Evelyn Waugh*
4. Remembrance of Things Past, Vol. 1   *Marcel Proust*
5. The Informed Heart   *Bruno Bettelheim*
6. The Seven Pillars of Wisdom   *T. E. Lawrence*
7. The Red and the Black   *Stendahl*
8. Alain on Happiness   *Alain*
9. The Magic Mountain   *Thomas Mann*
10. The Caine Mutiny   *Herman Wouk*

Reading While Taking a Bath

1. Our Mutual Friend   *Charles Dickens*
2. Memoirs of Hadrian   *Marguerite Yourcenar*
3. Madame Bovary   *Gustave Flaubert*
4. Nana   *Emile Zola*
5. Turn of the Screw   *Henry James*
6. Dubliners   *James Joyce*
7. Green Mansions   *W. H. Hudson*
8. Collected Stories of John O'Hara   *John O'Hara*
9. The Stories of John Cheever   *John Cheever*
10. Miss Lonelyhearts   *Nathanael West*

Reading in Bed

1. Obscure Destinies   *Willa Cather*
2. The Slave   *Isaac Bashevis Singer*
3. Arrow in the Blue   *Arthur Koestler*
4. Someone Like You   *Roald Dahl*
5. The Fifth Business   *Robertson Davies*
6. Herzog   *Saul Bellow*
7. The Lonely Passion of Judith Hearne   *Brian Moore*

8. The Cannibal Galaxy   *Cynthia Ozick*
9. King Solomon's Mines   *H. Rider Haggard*
10. In Bluebeard's Castle   *George Steiner*

Reading in the Country

1. The Bridge of San Luis Rey   *Thornton Wilder*
2. Barchester Towers   *Anthony Trollope*
3. Anna Karenina   *Leo Tolstoy*
4. Mrs. Dalloway   *Virginia Woolf*
5. The Trial   *Franz Kafka*
6. Tender Is the Night   *F. Scott Fitzgerald*
7. Sister Carrie   *Theodore Dreiser*
8. Candide   *Voltaire*
9. Grapes of Wrath   *John Steinbeck*
10. For Whom the Bell Tolls   *Ernest Hemingway*

Reading in a Plane or Train

1. Will's Boy   *Wright Morris*
2. The Moon and Sixpence   *W. Somerset Maugham*
3. Gift from the Sea   *Anne Morrow Lindbergh*
4. Siddhartha   *Hermann Hesse*
5. Ficciones   *Jorge Luis Borges*
6. Stories   *Katherine Mansfield*
7. The Screwtape Letters   *C. S. Lewis*
8. The Art of Loving   *Erich Fromm*
9. The Complete Sherlock Holmes   *Arthur Conan Doyle*
10. The Secret Agent   *Joseph Conrad*

Reading in a Garden

1. The Little Prince   *Antoine de Saint-Exupéry*

2. Hamlet: *William Shakespeare*
   Frailty, Thy Name Is Woman, Act I, Scene ii
   To Be or Not To Be, Act III, Scene i
3. King Lear: *William Shakespeare*
   Lear and Cordelia, Act I, Scene vii
4. "Crabbed Age and Youth" from
   The Passionate Pilgrim *William Shakespeare*
5. "Past Reason Hunted" from
   The Sonnets, CXXIX *William Shakespeare*
6. "Love's Philosophy" from
   Collected Poems of Shelley *Percy Bysshe Shelley*
7. Faust and Margaret, from
   Faust, Part One *J. W. von Goethe*
8. "A Parable" from *Collected Stories* *Oscar Wilde*
9. Martin Eden *Jack London*
10. Essays *Ralph Waldo Emerson*

Reading by the Lake

1. The Stranger *Abert Camus*
2. A High Wind in Jamaica *Richard Hughes*
3. Pericles' Funeral Oration *Thucydides*
4. The Colossus of Maroussi *Henry Miller*
5. A Separate Peace *John Knowles*
6. The Long Goodbye *Raymond Chandler*
7. The Liberal Imagination *Lionel Trilling*
8. The Basic Fault *Michael Balint*
9. The Wound and the Bow *Edmund Wilson*
10. Rubaiyat of Omar Khayyám
    Translated by *Edward Fitzgerald*

Reading When Bored

1. Modern Man in Search of a Soul *C. G. Jung*
2. Humboldt's Gift *Saul Bellow*

3. The Nine Tailors — *Dorothy Sayers*
4. The Daughter of Time — *Josephine Tey*
5. The Maltese Falcon — *Dashiell Hammett*
6. Travels in Arabia Deserta — *Charles M. Doughty*
7. Dr. Jekyll and Mr. Hyde — *Robert Louis Stevenson*
8. The Woman in White — *Wilkie Collins*
9. Robinson Crusoe — *Daniel Defoe*
10. Captain Horatio Hornblower — *C. S. Forester*

Reading in Search of Ideas

1. Island — *Aldous Huxley*
2. Job — *Old Testament*
3. Genesis — *Old Testament*
4. Corinthians — *New Testament*
5. Irrational Man — *William Barrett*
6. Beyond Good and Evil — *Friedrich Nietzsche*
7. Man's Search for Himself — *Rollo May*
8. Ideology and Utopia — *Karl Mannheim*
9. The Hero with a Thousand Faces — *Joseph Campbell*
10. The Varieties of Religious Experience — *William James*

Reading Just a Good Book

1. Middlemarch — *George Eliot*
2. Tom Jones — *Henry Fielding*
3. Man's Fate — *André Malraux*
4. Maldorer — *Comte de Lautreamont*
5. Bourgeois Anonymous — *Morris Philipson*
6. Civilization and Its Discontents — *Sigmund Freud*
7. The Confidential Clerk — *T. S. Eliot*
8. Quinlan's Key — *Sterling Quinlan*
9. Adventures of Huckleberry Finn — *Mark Twain*
10. Lolita — *Vladimir Nabokov*